T0278374

Praise for *Holy Runaways*

"Matthias Roberts looks at the perils and promises of belief, querying whether freedom can partner with the practice of religion. *Holy Runaways* is a testament to struggle, questioning, intelligence, intellectual exploration, and, finally, to the belief that faith without flourishing is a contradiction in terms. It holds a mirror up, asks what its reader sees, and offers pathways of safety, life, and freedom."

—Pádraig Ó Tuama, poet, host, and
author of *Poetry Unbound*

"With his gentle but compelling voice to soothe the injuries we have incurred along the way, Matthias Roberts invites us to see that when our faith changes, we are not running away from something but toward something better. Reading this book, you will find that what is on the other side is healthier, more whole, more embodied. What's more, you will discover that the struggle along the way can also be trusted."

—Hillary L. McBride, psychologist, researcher,
podcaster, mother, and author of
The Wisdom of Your Body

"For anyone who has a traumatic relationship to the often-toxic institution that is American Christianity, *Holy Runaways* is a book that will hold your hand and remind you that you aren't alone. Roberts shares his expertise in both psychology and theology with tenderness and care, holding space for our questions while giving us courage to keep moving toward the kind of love we've been hoping for. The stories and wisdom in this book will help us come home to ourselves and recognize that God (or The Sacred) was here all along, waiting in the wide world for us to learn to deeply love the runaways in ourselves and one another."

—Kaitlin B. Curtice, award-winning author of
Native and *Living Resistance*

"Wow, wow, wow. I didn't expect to find belonging in these pages, but I did. Nor did I imagine I'd find home, but I did. Matthias Roberts offers this precious gift with his wit and his wisdom, his gorgeous prose, and his tender care. His radiant and generous spirit shines in his candid storytelling. This book, like this human, is utterly beautiful."

—Jeff Chu, author of *Does Jesus Really Love Me?*
and coauthor of *Wholehearted Faith*

"The world has been aching for a guide to show us what true liberation looks like, at a time when so many of us find ourselves in exile but scared to become a true runaway. Lucky for us, Matthias Roberts has the humility, intelligence, clarity, wit, and story to give us such a guide. *Holy Runaways* is an instant classic to be shelved between C. S. Lewis and Gustavo Gutiérrez for modern books that will forever transform the church and the way we see God. I used to think doubt was the opposite of faith, but Roberts makes a case that certainty is its true enemy. This book is a gift for anyone who will never be certain but values love, adventure, passion, mystery, and truth a whole lot more."

—Mari Andrew, *New York Times*–bestselling author
of *Am I There Yet?* and *My Inner Sky*

"*Holy Runaways* is not a book—it is a manifesto for the many queer folks who need to know we are indeed holy, indeed beautiful, indeed adored, indeed lovable and loved. Matthias has gifted us with a love letter to our younger selves to remind us that in spite of the created reality of toxic narratives, the Divine made no mistakes with us."

—Jo Luehmann, host of *The Living Room* podcast

"As a holy runaway from the toxic religion of my past, I somehow lost myself in Matthias's poignant telling of his own story, and found myself at the same time as the truth of our common humanity resonated with my soul."

—Cindy Wang Brandt, author of *Parenting Forward* and *You Are Revolutionary*

"The internet is filled with former fundamentalists, exvangelicals, and post-Christian deconstructionists who will give you (compelling) reasons to leave the rigid religion of your childhood behind. Like them, Matthias Roberts has had to leave behind oppressive religious upbringing, and he refuses to shrink back from naming the many pitfalls and dangers of oppressive spirituality. But Roberts refuses only to curse the darkness, choosing also to light a path forward. *Holy Runaways* is a must-read for anyone who has been hurt by religious institutions but is looking to reconstruct a capacious, life-giving faith. A poignant book that arrives at just the moment it's most needed!"

—Jonathan Merritt, contributing writer for *The Atlantic* and author of *Learning to Speak God from Scratch*

"For all of us wandering zealots, now vagabonds finding our way through the wild wonders of faith and belief, Matthias Roberts has offered a light on the path in front of us with his gentle and beautiful guiding for the holy runaways in all of us. Roberts offers us the words that we who've been told we're on the outskirts of connection to the Divine most need: that we belong and we always have."

—Arielle Estoria, poet, actor, and author of *The Unfolding*

"Unapologetic. Deeply vulnerable. Validating. Unorthodox—in the most surprising and extraordinary ways. Life-giving, luminous, and liberating. The words in this book are exactly what so many of us holy runaways—the abandoned, ignored, forgotten—are running toward. Matthias asks himself, 'Was I hiding from the truth instead of shining a light on it?' The answer is, not at all. He's most beautifully shining a light on too many truths that have long been hidden."

—Marcie Alvis Walker, author of *Everybody Come Alive: A Memoir in Essays*

"Sometimes religion is the problem. Sometimes, our faith is broken by what we've been given, what we have inherited, and what is all around us. But tiny seeds of hope, light, and belonging help us continue on the way of rediscovering ourselves while we hold the paradox of faith in these moments. Embracing uncertainty and learning how to unravel from these harmful dogmatic systems is part of the work of becoming a holy runaway. I can only hope that my life mirrors the work of this book and encourages others to embrace the real work of faith in being rooted in yourself enough to become a holy runaway. Much praise for this book!"

—Roberto Che Espinoza, author of *Body Becoming* and *Activist Theology*

"As someone whose own runaway process hastened as a result of compassion toward a friend in the LGBTQ+ community, Matthias Roberts rightly notes that in relationship we cannot *not* change—even to the point of questioning what was once a sturdy foundation. As folks admit disillusionment with religion and seek something different, *Holy Runaways* offers a compassionate and nuanced approach of love, truth, and God. Roberts's emphasis on the complexity of disentangling faith, longing for certainty, and moving toward hope is welcoming and inspiring."

—Laura Anderson, founder and director of the Center for Trauma Resolution and Recovery, cofounder of the Religious Trauma Institute, and author of *When Religion*

Holy Runaways

Holy Runaways

Rediscovering Faith after
Being Burned by Religion

Matthias Roberts

Broadleaf Books
Minneapolis

Published in association with Gardner Literary, LLC. www.
gardner-literary.com.

Some names and details have been changed to protect the privacy of the
individuals involved. Conversations recounted from memory are expressed as
dialogue. The author has checked with sources believed to be reliable in his efforts
to provide information that is complete and generally in accord with standards
of practice that are accepted at the time of publication. However, in view of the
possibility of human error or changes in behavioral, mental health, or medical
sciences, neither the author, nor the editor and publisher, nor any other party who
has been involved in the preparation or publication of this work warrants that the
information contained herein is in every respect accurate or complete, and they are
not responsible for any errors or omissions or the results obtained from the use of
such information. Readers are encouraged to confirm the information contained in
this book with other sources.

By the sale of this book, neither the publisher nor the author is engaged in
rendering psychological or other professional services. If expert assistance or
counseling is needed, the services of a competent professional should be sought.

Library of Congress Control Number 2023005208

Cover design: 1517 Media

Print ISBN: 978-1-5064-8565-2
eBook ISBN: 978-1-5064-8566-9

Contents

Part 5
Slippery Slopes

Part 6
Pain

Part 7
Faith

Foreword

When I was 25 years old at the height of my own spiritual maturity (sic), my then husband and I took three hundred middle and high school students to New Mexico for youth camp. Evangelical Summer Youth Camp™ is its own ecosystem and deserves tomes of anthropological analysis to unpeel, but for our purposes here, the only detail I want you to know is that we took participating students on a guided whitewater rafting excursion one afternoon.

We were grouped and paired up with rafting guides, about six of us per raft. Outside of making sure an "adult" was in each group (in youth group late '90s, anyone north of prom was considered an adult), the rest of this dispersing was willy-nilly. I was placed with my best friend Jenny and a handful of rowdy boys.

Our guide was a six-foot, two-inch powerhouse named Sharon. She towered over all of us and was strong as an ox. Her confidence bolstered us, as we were a crew of diaper babies when it came to rapidly moving water and oars we were expected to man. We were in good hands, Sharon's hands, better than all our hands combined clearly. She'd rafted thousands of times; she'd seen things. She barked orders, and even the hardiest among us wouldn't dare disobey. "Do this, this, and this," Sharon commanded, "and never do this, this, or this." (The details elude me, but they seemed of utmost importance then.)

"Yes, Sharon," we replied like her sheeple.

I looked around at our squad of adolescents whose parents entrusted their well-being to us, and I wondered for the first but not last time if this was wise. Some of these children made elementary science fair projects last year. They had no hair under their arms. The oars were taller than half of them. Were their guides as capable as Sharon? They all looked like off-season ski instructors operating outside their primary ability so they wouldn't have to get real jobs in the summer. Of the lot of us, there were exactly six experts and thirty overconfident Texans (a redundant phrase).

Because I am not outdoorist, I can't remember what level the rapids were, but I can tell you this: we were immediately and urgently alarmed. This was not a slightly moving river fit for zealous young Baptists. This was a raging river. *Raging*, I tell you. We were dipping and crashing and screaming and spinning. My particular response to terror is to laugh hysterically, like one might do at a funeral after becoming unhinged. The teenagers were all panic-stricken while the youth pastor's wife cackled like a terrifying clown.

Sharon was our savior. She screamed instructions nonstop, and we did exactly as told because we were pro-life (wink). We corrected and steered, leaned backward in unison, kept our wits when wave after ice-cold wave broke over our entire raft. I have no idea how she kept us upright, but I have never obeyed someone with such diligence before or since, and I credit her alone with our 100 percent survival rate.

However, as we reached a calm section of the river first, I turned around to see how the rest of the children in our tender care had fared. Good reader, when I tell you the river was *teeming* with bobbing teen heads and distressed guides trying to get them back in the rafts, I mean to tell you that easily 75% of our charges had gone overboard and were shrieking like banshees. They were clinging to rocks, swimming hopelessly against the current, and screaming for the angels to save them. It was an unmitigated disaster. By the grace of Mary Mother of Jesus, there were no cell phones yet, so this was undocumented and certainly polished up in the retelling. How did any youth pastors in the '90s stay out of jail?

I have a point.

You are the lucky reader about to begin Matthias's gorgeous book, and I couldn't be more thrilled for you. I simply cannot add one decent word to what he has already penned. His story and storytelling abilities supersede mine by a factor of infinity. Matthias will, in concert, work through pain, fear, courage, healing, empathy, injustice, theology, identity, suffering, faith, and many, many, many metaphors, which delights me to no end. There is nothing to bolster. His work is complete and beautiful.

Here is what I can offer: when wading through such tumultuous waters, you are required to choose a good guide. These are not easy spaces to maneuver; in fact, many travelers have capsized in these tributaries. You need a steady hand, a safe and knowledgeable voice, someone who has completed thousands of these passages. You want a guide who has been there, who can tell you what is around the bend, point out that one rock that derailed many a hopeful adventurer.

I am here as a character witness. You have chosen the best guide. Matthias is everything I crave in a leader: gentle yet principled, smart as a damn whip, humble and generous, "pastoral" in the best ways and none of the bad. I have loved and admired him for years. I've learned to trust his measured response when everyone else's hair is on fire. He settles me, if that makes any sense. He is trustworthy, and that matters.

You will hear him pour his heart out to you in these pages. Matthias is equal parts vulnerable and wise—it is sometimes hard to be both at once. His experiences have been proven in the very real world, so don't mistake him for a removed academic. He gives it all to us in this book with a generosity of spirit that will assuredly make you cry before you close the last page.

Oh! Please be so excited because there is so much hope here. More than you even dared wish for perhaps. Your pain will find a soft place to land here, of course, but bring your tender heart as well because the hopefulness will win the day. I like this. I like this way of being in the world, which is precisely why I love Matthias Roberts like a dear brother.

Welcome, reader. You are in for some rapids—you are already in them, of course, because life is like that—but your guide will lead you through with a kindhearted, steady hand. Matthias's story is his, not exactly like yours or mine, and this book is not a prescription or template, but may you find your reflection in these pages in a way that affirms your own innate belovedness, celebrates your worthiness, and leads you to a calm section of the river.

With great love,
Jen Hatmaker

Author's Note
A Word about Pain

If you've picked up this book, you've probably been wounded by Christianity, and you're trying to figure out what to do with that pain, perhaps how to work with it and gain strength and perspective from the healing process.

But I need to warn you that reading this book may hurt.

In fact, you might need to stop as you read some passages. In this book, I pull out Bible verses, mention Jesus often, and share many anecdotes that may press on the wounds you're trying to heal.

I hope the way I approach these topics will help wrap language around your pain like a healing bandage. But it could as easily go the other way. It might feel like taking sandpaper to your already bleeding skin.

If I saw you in real life rubbing sandpaper on your bleeding wounds, I'd gently step in to ask why you're using something abrasive to try to heal yourself. With that in mind, I hope you will pause at any point when this book is bringing you that kind of pain and ask yourself the same question: Why are you trying to use sandpaper to heal?

Yes, pain is often part of the process of healing, but there's a difference between the kind of pain that comes when our bodies are healing and the kind of pain that causes more damage. I trust your ability to discern the difference.

If this book looks like a block of sandpaper to you when you open it, please put it down and find a bandage instead. If that means walking away from your faith completely, may you do so with blessing.

To those of you who don't have wounds or scars but are reading this book for other reasons: Welcome. If you're hoping to learn from a new perspective and deepen your ability to empathize with others, I hope *Holy Runaways* offers you some insight and ways to connect with those who have been hurt by religious institutions and people. Just remember that throughout the book, I'll be talking directly to those who bear the scars, but I'm glad you're listening too.

Let's begin.

Introduction

When I was little, I thought there was something romantic and magical about running away.

In the Northwoods of Wisconsin, where my parents worked at a large Christian camp, my sisters, other staff members' kids, and I often wandered off into the woods to play some variation of a runaway game.

"Let's pretend we're orphans running away from the evil orphanage keeper."

"You be the mean mom, and the rest of us will run away!"

We spent hours pretending we were running, hiding, and creating a new home. A new world where we would be safe from all the evil adults.

Not that any of the adults in our lives were particularly evil. But we were raised on *The Boxcar Children*, *Annie*, and *A Little Princess*. Those stories captured our imaginations, bringing faraway worlds of risk and survival to life. The kids in those stories braved all odds to pull through on their own, to get away from the "bad guys" who pursued them. And after they made their great escapes, the kids in the pages of our books somehow created homey comfort in beds of moss and within walls of woven sticks.

Later, after my family moved to Iowa when I was ten, to a spot of land surrounded by cornfields, I announced loudly to my parents at least a half dozen times, "I'm running away!"

I'd pack a bag—a change of clothes, fresh underwear, and a water bottle—and stomp out of the house, my mom always handing me a snack or two just before I slammed the door.

I usually did my running in the winter. I'm really not sure why, and in retrospect, it would have been more strategic to run during the long, warm summer days. But in those rebellious moods, thinking critically was the last thing my mind could handle. I was already anxious about resisting my parents' expectations, already understanding that I was supposed to fit into a pretty narrow box that defined exactly what a good Christian kid should do and say.

I had different, bigger plans.

"I'll show them! I'll go become famous. Like Amy Grant."

I'd traipse over frozen ground, my breath visible in clouds in front of me as I huffed out all the frustration in my little body. I always headed toward the huge empty metal grain bins on the other side of the property we lived on. It was a good place to set up home base while I figured out how to get to a recording studio.

Once inside, I'd brush aside the thin layer of corn or soybeans that still littered the floors from the fall harvest and dream about finding parents who would let me do whatever I wanted—and of my new life as a Christian pop artist.

Every time I sat alone on that cold, dusty floor, I talked through pros and cons, reasoning with myself out loud. And every time, I finally decided I did actually *like* my parents. And they weren't actually evil.

Maybe, I told myself, I was the bad one because I had abandoned them, abandoned my home.

As I looked around the ice-cold stainless-steel walls, I thought maybe not being allowed to paint my room a color other than white wasn't so bad after all. String by string, the cheese sticks my mom had handed me disappeared, and so did my confidence. What was I going to do for food on the way to Los Angeles or New York or Nashville? I couldn't eat the grains of corn scattered in front of me.

I usually endured the cold until my ears felt tingly (no annoying hats or earmuffs allowed in my new world of freedom).

And eventually, I ran home and through the back door just in time to take my seat at the kitchen table for dinner.

Another runaway attempt thwarted—but the allure remained.

It still remains.

Now in my thirties, I sometimes nurse the hope of something different, something better, all easily within my grasp by just running away from the current dull, white box I'm in. Why not get a fresh start? Drop all the trappings of my ordinary life and suddenly become something new. Someone different and better, with different and better problems.

These days, I mostly imagine dropping everything and moving to a new city. When life gets particularly hard, or when I'm feeling particularly lonely or misunderstood, I'll start dreaming and googling. Maybe Denver or Minneapolis. Or maybe back to that little town in Arkansas where I went to college. Oh, look at all the things I could afford far from the West Coast. Look at this charming house I could buy for less than I pay for rent in Seattle. I could drive an Audi. I'd be so much cooler there. Everything would be better. Wouldn't it?

I don't think I'm alone in these fantasies. I don't have any data to back this up, but have you ever noticed the only show HGTV ever seems to play anymore is some version of *House Hunters*? And all those texts I get from friends—maybe you get them too—imagining sharing a condo they found in Puerto Vallarta or dreaming of being able to afford to remodel a chateau in France, like people they stumbled across on social media. They're clearly thinking the same thing—how nice it would be to escape. We'd all be wearing loose white linen clothing and laughing into the sunset.

Yes, I know. There's the fantasy of running away, and then there's real life—when you run out of cheese sticks.

I imagine you can think of moments in your past when you have become a runaway, when you packed your bags and jumped in the car or bought a bus ticket. Maybe your decision was suddenly forced upon you, and you didn't even have time to pack a bag.

We all run away, whether from our jobs, our hometowns, or our families. We leave marriages, friendships, and church communities.

In this book, I'm going to talk about how and why we leave our faith and what happens afterward.

As a therapist, I often listen to people tell their stories of running away, and I almost always hear them talk about a nagging question echoing in their heads: Is it me? Is there something wrong with me? Am I the bad one for trying to run away?

Just like I thought I must be a bad son for thinking about leaving my parents as a ten-year-old. Just like I was sure I was a bad Christian for thinking about leaving my church when I was in my twenties.

Do you hear those questions echoing in your mind too, with their anxious follow-ups: *Is this suffering I'm experiencing really something I deserve? Are they all right, and I'm all wrong? Maybe all I need to do is change myself, to make myself fit in better?*

Or, most painfully: *What did I do wrong to make it all go bad?*

There's a yearning in those kinds of questions. A yearning for things to go back to *normal*. Back to what they were. A yearning to return home to a familiar kitchen table and a familiar family around it.

Each of us runs away in our unique ways, but in the past several years, I've heard more and more stories of people who grew up like me—white suburban church kids who are running from their spiritual homes and asking strikingly similar questions. Really big questions like: *What happened to the world? What happened to the ideals I learned about in Sunday school? Is this faith in which I once felt comfortable and protected now a tool of oppression and hatred?*

In the past few years, people of my generation have watched over 80 percent of our peers, our parents, and the people who babysat us vote against almost every value we were taught, including compassion, kindness, empathy, and love.

And we have heard those people insist that *we're* the ones who don't understand.

We have struggled to make sense of it, and if you're anything like me, you've been completely baffled. Most days feel as if the world has flipped on its head. We're being told right is wrong, evil is actually good, and Jesus's instruction to love thy neighbor meant it's okay to throw kids in cages while singing the national anthem.

Then, speechless, we watched people we love vote for it all again.

Now, as I write this, it feels as if we're waking up from a weird dream and seeing our surroundings with new eyes. What was once a place of safety, goodness, and so-called purity—a place we called home—has turned out to be a place of harm.

There were good parts in our past, yes indeed. But almost everyone I know has trauma, whether subtle or overt, lodged in our bodies. When we try to talk about it, someone inevitably shuts us down, yells at us, gaslights us. Someone else inevitably steps in and says we need to repent and get back onto the narrow path to salvation.

It's confusing, to say the least.

How do we find home when our homes have shapeshifted into sinister haunted houses we don't recognize? When we have opened our eyes from the dream to find ourselves in a wilderness—but it doesn't feel like we've actually moved?

Some people call this process of realization and questioning of faith *deconstruction*, and I don't mind that term.

But I prefer to see myself and others as runaways. Whether we were cast out or have run away on our own volition, we are not going blindly. We are all looking for something.

Most of us runaways have tasted deep *goodness*, and we want to taste it again. We have told ourselves wonderful stories and spent years imagining how different life could be. We want more; we want better.

A place to rest. A place to call home.

So many people I know are in this in-between, running-away place when it comes to their faith. So many of my clients in my small therapy practice are wrestling with questions that, in one way or another, amount to: *How do we find our home again?*

If any of what I've said so far resonates with you, I want you to hear this: I think we are more than just confused, fearful, or misguided runaways. I think we are *holy*.

Not holy in that stuffy church pew kind of way. But holy in that we are not settling, not satisfied, but always seeking to transcend. We're setting ourselves apart, searching for something different and better that reflects our faith instead of twisting or mocking it. And ultimately, we are asking our faith to do more about the violence and pain in the world than simply offering thoughts and prayers for victims.

It usually feels awful and painful to leave everything we know behind. But it becomes easier if we know that in our searching, we're doing something natural, something quintessentially human, and something that reveals the divine spark in each of us. This quest is something we are all meant to do.

We're holy runaways.

Part 1

Mustard Seeds

Cracks

I took the first small step on my holy runaway journey while sitting in a cathedral pew.

At my Christian college, we were required to go to chapel twenty-one times per semester. If we didn't, we would be put on probation. I was a rule follower, so that was never a problem for me.

But one day, the president of the university was speaking at the cathedral. He was a kind man, at least on the surface, one who seemed to embrace nuance and complexity. He stood on the chapel stage of this Christian school and implored students not to use the word *gay* in a derogatory way because we could never know who in the room was struggling with feelings of same-sex attraction. I appreciated that because I was one of those people. And the way the word was tossed around by some of my peers hurt.

Every time the topic came up in chapel, I paid a little bit more attention while also attempting to look a little bit less like I was paying attention. I didn't want anyone to know I was one of those people.

I can't remember his exact words that day, but I do remember their results. The president was calling us as a college community, a Christian community, to be compassionate and kind to people like me. People like me, who would spend their entire lives alone because being in a relationship wasn't an option.

That was the official university position.

For these people, he said, it was okay to struggle with same-sex attraction. But to act on the attraction was a sin. It was our duty, *my* duty, to embrace a life alone.

The president, with what I imagine he believed were wholly good intentions and a soft, forgiving tone, asked the student body to be the kind of people who would walk alongside their struggling siblings. And then he reaffirmed the official university position on LGBTQ+ relationships—that there couldn't be any.

Everyone around me began to clap; some cheered. They cheered because it sounded good, like a challenge. And they were all up for the challenge of being good friends to people like me without compromising on the truth of God's design.

I shifted uncomfortably in my seat and didn't clap. To me, it sounded like they were cheering for me to be lonely for the rest of my life.

And something in me cracked.

I had the urge to run away, an urge I hadn't felt so strongly since I was a kid back in Iowa.

I didn't pack my bags or drop out. Remember, I was a rule follower. But those cheers began to reverberate inside me, making me wonder if I actually belonged.

Bigger

Get ready because now I'm going to talk about Jesus.

Before you skip this chapter or put this book down forever, let me tell you that I don't really care what you think about Jesus. Not because I think I'm right and you're wrong, and not because it doesn't matter what you think, but because you are welcome to bring all your faith, doubts, fears, and uncertainty about Jesus to this book. Whether you believe he was human or divine; that his mother, Mary, was a virgin; or he really came back from the dead—none of that matters when it comes to what I'm sharing here.

I'll start with a Bible story—maybe you've heard it before. It's from Matthew 17:14–20.

Some of Jesus's disciples came to him distraught one day because they believed they had failed. A man had approached them and asked if they could cure his son. The disciples had tried to help the child, but it didn't work.

The man decided to go to the top, following the disciples to Jesus and begging him to intervene.

"Your disciples couldn't cure my son. Can you?" the man asked.

Jesus got frustrated—a response I've always found odd. He spoke some choice words, wondering how much longer he had to put up with these "faithless" people. Then he healed the kid instantly, right in front of the disciples.

"Why couldn't *we* heal him? What did we do wrong?" asked one of the disciples.

Jesus answered quietly, "Because you have so little faith."

I imagine that stung a bit, don't you? They must have been thinking, *Come on, Jesus—we literally gave up our lives to follow you.*

But Jesus ignored the pained looks on their faces and kept talking, sharing an idea you've probably heard in church and Sunday school: *If you have faith the size of a mustard seed, you will say to this mountain, "Move from here to there," and it will move; and nothing will be impossible for you.*[1]

I grew up hearing this story many times, and I always understood it as an indictment of weakness, including my own.

When I went to Colorado for the first time as a ten-year-old, I sat in the far back seat of the family van, looked at a mountain, and said, "Move over there!"

I don't know what I was expecting. I was from the flatlands. I had never seen a mountain before. But a part of me was hoping it would move.

It didn't.

So I added, "In the name of *Jesus*, move!"

It still didn't move.

I need you to understand that I was saying this all in my head. No matter how religious my family was, I wasn't about to start talking to a mountain in front of them. But you better believe that when we got out of that van and I was alone, I tried again, this time out loud. That had to be the missing piece of the incantation, I thought.

There were no news reports that day, or any day, of a mountain outside of Delta, Colorado, relocating.

I wondered if my faith wasn't even as big as a mustard seed. Maybe I didn't have any faith. Maybe there was something wrong with me.

I wondered how to make my faith *bigger*. Big enough to move a mountain. My faith needed to be more. Different. Better.

As I studied the parable of the mustard seed later, I realized that the boy Jesus healed wasn't just a boy. He was a member of a complex system made up of family, community, and a larger culture of norms and expectations. And I imagine that system was in chaos by the time the boy's father approached the disciples.

He had told the disciples his son often fell, and he fell not just on the ground but into fire and water. That sounds terrifying. That's the kind of thing that would change a family and potentially even a community. People all around them would be forever watching out for this kid and waiting for disaster to strike. That's what drove the father to ask for some miraculous healing.

The disciples tried to fix the system, to restore order, to put things back the way they should be. But they couldn't. They failed.

I know that feeling. I've sat in with communities—both my own and not my own—and tried to fix them. I've looked at people who seemed possessed by their strong beliefs, people who were causing harm, and said to them, "Let me help you get better." I've never offered miracles but have tried so hard, over long periods of time, until I've finally thrown up my hands in exasperation and said, "Maybe it'll never get better."

I've walked away—hurt, ego deflated—wondering if I was asking for too much but also thinking maybe *I* was the problem. *Maybe, like the disciples, I don't have enough faith.*

The disciples went to Jesus after he performed the healing and wanted answers: "Why couldn't we do it? Why couldn't we heal this child?"

"You couldn't do it because you had too little faith" was his answer. And he added, as if to taunt or tease them a little, "But all you need is faith the size of a small seed."

Thanks, Jesus.

Exodus

They say the church is dying. That if no one does something about it, the church as we know it is going to disappear. They have numbers to prove it. Church attendance among adults in the United States has declined significantly in the past decade.[1] People are leaving individual churches of all denominations in droves.

They ask, "Why is this happening? How can we reach the younger generations?"

Many researchers and analysts have tried to answer those questions for years. Books on the topic pile up on library shelves, and op-eds are offered to the masses. Some say we need to return to biblical teachings, that the church's Truth™ has been watered down by our twenty-first-century culture. People may not like the Truth, but we must stand for something, they argue, and speaking our Truth is the only way God will provide a revival.

Traditional values will save us all. Amen.

Other people are working on repackaging their faith, making their messaging friendlier, casting aside the image of a God who wants to judge the world and replacing it with someone you might want to have a drink with.

There's a church in Seattle that meets at a bar so you can sip a mimosa while listening to the morning sermon. It's called Bar Church. I went one time and then decided if I was gonna do brunch, I might as well just do *actual* brunch.

Everyone has an idea about how to revive the church and bring people back. And yet the question grows louder year after year: "How can we bring in the younger generation?"

But every year, more people run away.

If you're reading this, I'm guessing you're one of those people. Or you're at least considering making your escape. I bet you also have some ideas about why people are running away.

But why are *you* running? What would your church, your pastor, your community have to do to be worthy of your return?

As a runaway myself, I've thought a lot about these questions, and I believe most people are running because they're finding God elsewhere. They've discovered, as I did, that God is bigger than what's inside the four walls of any church.

A lot of people, including me, are also running because the God summoned and discussed within the four walls of their church seems like an asshole, and they don't want anything to do with a God like that.

Or maybe they're running because none of it makes sense.

That's what I was thinking on the day my college president told my friends to be kind to me because I'd never be loved the way I wanted to be loved, and I'd be alone forever.

Before I went off to college, I pitied the people who ran away from our church community. I thought it was sad, as if they didn't have enough willpower. Or maybe Satan jumped out of the bushes one night and got them. Or they were never real Christians at all.

"That's so *sad*," I would say, patting myself on the back for not being like them. At least *I* was okay.

But that was before the crack opened inside me.

Watching and listening to all my friends cheer and applaud for my loneliness, congratulating themselves for the charity of being a good friend to me despite who I was, changed me.

I didn't take a generous view of the people in the cathedral that day. They didn't know their cheers were about me—but

I knew. And in those cheers and murmurs, I heard the same kind of pity I had felt in the past for the people who ran away.

Now I was on the receiving end, and it didn't feel good.

Looking back, I can see how angry I was and how hard it was to hide that anger. I didn't want the friendship of the people in the pews that day—friendship offered with a gentle smile and a pat on the head.

"I'm so sorry you have to be alone your whole life," they'd say, "but can I buy you coffee?"

I didn't want that brand of kindness. I wanted a partner. A husband. And so I started to look for God elsewhere.

And eventually, I found her.

A Kiss

When I realized that God could be found on the lips of another man, I was surprised—but maybe not that surprised. I had crossed a line, a line I was told I should never, *ever* cross—and to my surprise, God was there waiting for me.

Suddenly, God was bigger and more beautiful, expanding beyond the images that had constrained my thinking as a child and a young man, and it felt perfectly normal.

Just like that. With one kiss.

People like you and me are running away from the church because we realize its walls are too confining. And soon after we start running, we discover God is out there beyond the walls, just waiting for us.

But if God is alive beyond the church's walls, what do we do with all the churches and all the walls?

People who use the word *deconstruction* to describe their process of questioning their faith sometimes talk about disassembling the walls, stripping everything down to the foundation. It's a helpful metaphor in some ways, but my own experience was less like demolition and more like looking back to see the walls were cracked but still intact, held up by the people who remained inside.

It's kind of like that story of the little Dutch boy who discovered a hole in the levy. Water was spilling through it, so this kid plugged it with his finger.

But then another hole popped up, so he plugged that one with another finger. And another hole opened, but he couldn't do anything about that one. A villager was walking by and came over to plug up the third hole. Soon, the entire village was at the levy, plugging holes with their fingers, trying to make sure it didn't collapse. For all I know, they're still there to this day.

For all I know, they call themselves a church.

When I found God on the lips of a man, I decided I should just let go of holding up those walls and walk away. At first, I took only a few steps, the start of a long journey.

And when I looked back, all I could see were the cracks, the holes, and the people furiously trying to cover them.

I tried to shout back at some of those people I cared about. "Hey, God is over here too. Maybe you're keeping out the Holy Spirit by plugging those cracks," I said. "The Spirit is over here, beyond the walls, and there's nothing to be afraid of!"

The opening I had climbed through was quickly covered up, so my voice couldn't reach the people still inside.

But I could hear the murmurs continuing to rumble through the air: "We lost another one!" "How do we save the church?" "How do we keep the young people?"

I shook my head and took a few more steps. They were all wrong. I wasn't lost; I had found something. Something as refreshing and comforting as a warm evening breeze.

But I was also confused.

Fakes

I imagine Jesus's disciples were confused, too, when he told them they only needed faith the size of a mustard seed. The no-nonsense Bible authors don't really linger on this story—as if it's self-explanatory: *Have faith like a mustard seed. Move mountains. Nothing will be impossible for you.*

Boom, end of story. Go have fun now.

How could that be a sufficient answer to the disciples' profound questions about their failure to heal something that was broken, someone who was hurting?

It sounded like what the people inside the walls had often said to me:

"You just need more faith."

"Don't give up on God."

"Nothing is impossible for those who believe, so you'd better get back here and start believing."

Those responses never made me feel like anyone was really listening to me. They made me want to run away faster and farther. I wanted to yell louder, to drown them out:

"Can't you see this is broken?"

"Can't you see this is not what it should be?"

"Can't you see the ways you are hurting people?"

"Can't you see *me*?"

I wanted these people who claimed to be like Jesus to actually *be* like Jesus. But instead, they parroted Jesus's words. They were cheap fakes. Weren't they?

The darker fear in my head was hard to face, so I hid from it for a long time: maybe Jesus actually was like them.

Faithless

I've often been struck by how angry Jesus gets in the mustard seed story.

He gets angry at the disciples when he hears they couldn't cure the boy, couldn't heal the system.

"You faithless and perverse generation," says Jesus. "How much longer must I be with you? How much longer must I put up with you?"[1]

These are familiar words, aren't they? *Faithless. Perverse.*

Maybe Jesus is like all those voices in my life, I thought.

Or maybe Jesus was saying something else, doing something else.

The disciples were runaways too, weren't they? A bunch of people who dropped everything, ran away from all they knew to follow this intriguing, charismatic man named Jesus, a man who spoke of love and *home*. It takes some deep kind of faith to do that, and unless Jesus was completely oblivious, which he wasn't, that wouldn't have been lost on him.

Early in my own time as a runaway, I began to wonder if Jesus got angry at the disciples in this story because he actually *saw* their faith. He knew it was there. The word Jesus uses when he calls them "perverse" is *diastrepho*, which roughly means "to turn away."

His disciples had turned away from something.

I think Jesus could see these men had turned away from what was *inside them*, the faith that was already there, the pure faith that had led them away from their communities and into his service.

That turning away from their early faith frustrated Jesus. Instead of anger *at* them, I think he expressed his anger *on behalf* of them, on behalf of what they could have been had they been true to themselves.

Perhaps he was saying, "When will you see what I see? When will you trust what is inside you? You couldn't heal this boy because you didn't *believe* you could. You gave up. You didn't have faith in your God-given abilities."

Maybe he was acknowledging that he knew the disciples felt hopeless in that situation, that they had lost faith they could do anything at all. But I wonder if he was also telling them that he *saw* their faith, that it was still in there. They could tap into it—and they didn't need much.

I also wonder if in that passage, Jesus is talking to runaways today, us cynics who can't help but hope. Those of us who feel beaten down when our attempts to heal ourselves and our communities don't work.

Those of us who have felt something crack open inside us, like I did.

Worthiness

I can hardly go a day in my conversations with clients and friends without mentioning researcher and storyteller Brené Brown. She studies shame and vulnerability, and her work changed my life.

A few years ago, I picked up her book *The Gifts of Imperfection*. On page 23 of the old paperback I've marked up and dog-eared, she shares her experience researching human relationships and people who experience a strong sense of love and belonging.

I remember reading this section of the book for the first time and thinking: *This is what I need. I want to feel I am loved, to feel I belong.*

There are only two paragraphs on page 23. And in the first one, she drops a bomb.

She says only *one* thing separates those who have a strong sense of love and belonging from those who struggle with it: "That one thing is the belief in their worthiness. It's as simple and as complicated as this."[1]

Oh, okay, yes, let me go just dip into my bag of belief over here and pull out more worthiness.

Not that Brené Brown is Jesus (although I wouldn't be surprised), but for me, her statement has the same energy and subtext as Jesus's mustard seed story.

In different ways, they both say that what holds us back from experiencing love and belonging and faith to move mountains is *our lack of belief in our own worthiness.*

Reading Dr. Brown soon after I took the first steps on my runaway journey sent me into a tailspin. How could I just start believing I was worthy? I took a long hard look at myself and realized, deep down, she was right. I believed I was unworthy and that any sense of love or belonging I had was a gift given to me—a kindness from other people but a kindness that was just a form of pity.

That same kind of pity that set me on edge back in college in the cathedral pew.

The truth is that it's hard—really hard—to change our beliefs about ourselves. I run into this with my clients frequently, and I run into it with myself even more often. Because most of our beliefs about ourselves we take as absolute truth; we feel them in our bones. These beliefs feel deeper than mere thoughts.

I find myself often getting frustrated with people in my life who resist seeing things the way I do.

At times, I just want to yell at a friend, "Can't you see what I see? How much longer do I have to put up with you, with this? Can't you see you already have this power and greatness inside you?"

It's so much easier to see another person's worthiness than to believe in our own.

I wonder if that's what was happening for Jesus when he got angry. Maybe he could see something the disciples couldn't.

He could see their faith, their *worthiness*, their ability to heal. It was *in them*, but they were having a hard time finding it, despite being shown again and again. I think it was as simple and as complicated as this.

Sound familiar?

Tiny Hope

I'm quite aware of those worksheets and methodologies that promise if we just target the right self-limiting thoughts and the irrational beliefs we hold, confronting them with something more rational, something truer, we can be on our happy way into the future. Maybe you've tried those exercises too?

Sometimes they work in the short term. But in my experience, those exercises don't go deep enough. They don't get at the fundamental problem.

We're talking about core stuff here. Core stuff doesn't just change by thinking. Core stuff changes through a complicated combination of new and different experiences. And new and different experiences are hard to come by.

Jesus told his disciples the real truth about their faith, but they needed more experiences and couldn't understand the words.

"You couldn't heal because you didn't have faith. Yet it doesn't take much," he told them. "You don't have to fully believe. You don't even need *more* faith. If even a minuscule seed's worth is there, you can do the impossible."

If your runaway journey has been anything like mine up until this point, you have lost a lot of your early faith—and for good reasons. To continue in a faith journey feels impossible, like yelling back into a void. It feels hopeless, and you think it may be better to give up.

And yet—

I suspect a part of you *does* believe, *does* hope. The part of you that at this point probably feels foolish or naive. That part of you believes home is out there, rest is out there and hopes that maybe someday you can stop running. That's the part of you that still has a little faith.

Maybe that part is tiny—as tiny as a mustard seed. That might be all you need, all we need, to do what in this moment seems impossible.

Part 2

Concrete Boxes

Sand

There's another short story in the Bible—really, just a simple metaphor—in which Jesus compares two people. One person builds a house on a rock, and the other builds a house on sand. We would sing about those two builders in Sunday school:

The rains came down, and the floods came up!
The rains came down, and the floods came up!
The rains . . .

You get it.

And the house on the rock stood firm. The house on the sand fell down.

It's a good metaphor.

"Oh, that foolish man," my friends and I laughed, "doesn't he know houses on sand can't stand?"

My Sunday school teachers would explain that we weren't really talking about building houses but about how we should build our beliefs, our faith.

"Make sure you build your faith on a firm foundation!"

We all nodded and smiled. We were no fools.

Many of the people I talk to in my practice as a therapist are, like me, second-guessing their own faith. We want to believe; in fact, we yearn for faith. We search for it. We have a sense there is something larger, something cosmic, something divine in the universe. We want to step into a faith that confirms what we hope is true: the greatest of all things is love.

We want to believe God, or the Divine, or whatever is out there is Love.

And yet we're also questioning the massive disconnect between who our faith communities say they are and what they are doing in the world. We see questions of integrity at stake. How can the faithful hear Jesus's words about caring for other people and not act on them?

Looking at the church as it stands, built by generations before us, we now see all the cracks and gaping holes, and we are asking a new, troubling question: Is it possible that maybe they—maybe we—built this structure all wrong?

I have heard runaways like myself pose that question over and over. I now think that asking such questions may be our mission—a sacred mission.

Who better to ask difficult questions about the church's building materials and internal systems, policies, and responsibilities than those who have been on the inside? Who better to ask questions about the structural integrity of the church than those of us who have been burned by its lack of integrity?

Beyond the songs and metaphors, we need to understand what makes up the foundation and the walls that are supposed to protect us but often painfully confine us in the church.

Well, obviously, Jesus is our foundation, right? Even as runaways, most of us are still following Jesus, still believe in Jesus, don't we?

I still believe in Jesus. Don't I?

Let's assume for the moment our foundation has remained intact, and we still believe in Jesus and his teachings—the heart of Christianity. Unfortunately, that isn't enough to answer all our questions. Our Sunday school teachers, pastors, and parents didn't prepare us to cope with all the ugly cracks in the walls of our faith.

When I felt a warm breeze and saw God outside clearly crumbling church walls, I was afraid. It seemed threatening and disorienting. I first tried to cover my eyes and then covered the holes and turned away.

If you're like me that was your first response: Ignore it. Nothing to see here.

But we couldn't ignore all those cracks forever.

When we reached out in confusion and distress, loud voices responded, "You must have built your house on sand." The voices were so loud they drowned out any other responses that might have been more understanding or helpful. They drowned out our pain and hurt as they begged—or demanded—that we agree with them. And the voices were familiar—they were our pastors, friends, and family.

I don't think I understood at the time that none of them was really listening to us. Instead, they diagnosed and offered an impossible prescription to ease our pain.

"Nothing is wrong here, so it must be a problem with you. Have you tried reinforcing your foundation?"

The Gathering

If you had asked me back when I was sitting in that cathedral pew, before I even knew I was on a runaway journey, I would've told you my faith was pretty solid. I wasn't self-righteous, just surer of my own beliefs than I would be a few years later. At that point in college, I was too enmeshed in my "struggle with same-sex attraction" to feel self-righteous. No, that's not the truth—I often looked down on LGBTQ+ people I read about who left their religious communities to seek freedom. And I was self-righteously proud I wasn't one of them.

Because I felt the pain of this thorn in my flesh on a daily basis, I certainly thought I was working with a mustard plant-size faith instead of a little seed. Granted, my faith probably looked different from that of my friends and family, but I saw it as a lifeline and something that defined me.

Every Sunday night at 9:00 p.m., my college held a special chapel service called "The Gathering." Because it was late at night, most faculty and staff didn't attend, and the service was edgier—with louder worship music, including Top 40 hits with lyrics cleverly rearranged to be about Jesus. A student who was about to graduate delivered the sermon. It was a rite of passage. All seniors were given the opportunity to speak at The Gathering, which was a chance to cement your reputation as one of the Good Students, a credit to your class and the college.

Because of how involved I had been in student leadership on campus throughout my time there, it was a given that I would speak in The Gathering at some point.

As the weeks of junior year rolled by, I heard the questions more and more often from my friends and classmates: "Are you speaking at The Gathering next year, Matthias?" "Getting excited about your talk?"

I began to think that stage would be the perfect opportunity to share the secret about myself I had been holding inside for so long. I would come out to the whole student body, but it wouldn't be just about me. In coming out, I'd be able to humanize and personalize this abstract issue that had been a hot topic of debate around campus throughout my time there.

I wanted all the students to imagine *my* face, not some faceless stranger, the next time they applauded for loneliness. I also wanted to share what I had learned about God through my struggle and my choice to remain single for the rest of my life. I had a lot to say, and I liked the idea of a captive audience. I felt more excitement than fear as I sent the college chaplain my application to speak at the end of my junior year.

"Because of the topic matter of what you're wanting to share about" the email from the chaplain read, "the Office of Christian Formation would like you to write a word-for-word transcript of what you plan to say."

Well, that was kind of weird. I hadn't heard of anyone else having to write a transcript, but maybe I wasn't aware of a new policy. I asked around. Sure enough, everyone else who had spoken recently only had to submit sparse outlines.

Okay, I thought, *my subject is sensitive and sure to create controversy. Maybe they just want to be prepared for that.*

At that point, I was always willing to give people in authority the benefit of the doubt. I reasoned that my speech may have reminded the chaplain of the time another student had "come out" in an op-ed in the student newspaper. The author said he wanted to humanize LGBTQ+ people but at the end of the piece revealed it was a ploy—a lie. He was straight after all. He just wanted us to imagine what it would be like if someone on campus came out. The administration gave the student and the newspaper staff a lot of heat for that trick.

For weeks during my summer break, I worked on my speech in every spare moment I had. I tried to make sure it was not too shocking, integrated plenty of Scripture, and reassured anyone listening that while I was gay, I had never even held hands with a man, so I was Okay. Still Good. Still doing right by the church and the university.

I sent in the draft, and a few weeks passed. When they announced the speaker lineup for the fall semester, I wasn't on it.

Strange, I thought, still wanting to understand their point of view. Maybe they were just deliberating.

Halfway through the semester, I followed up. The chaplain told me the school's president had caught wind of my plan and requested the transcript. It might take another month or two, but if all went well, the chaplain assured me I would be able to speak in the spring.

Now that it seemed like a sure thing, I was suddenly nervous. What were people going to think of me? All at once, hundreds of my classmates and dozens of my friends were going to find out they'd been hanging out with someone who had been gay all along but had never told them. Would anyone still want to be my friend?

I'd heard a few stories about antigay violence on other Christian campuses. I began to wonder whether I would have to endure bullying or isolation if they didn't receive my speech in the way I intended. At least, I rationalized, I'd have only two or three months left before graduation.

Finally, at the beginning of the spring term, I got my email from the chaplain and prepared to circle the date on my calendar.

The president doesn't think our campus is ready for someone to come out yet, so for your protection, we've decided to not feature you as a Gathering speaker this year. Thanks for applying.

My stomach dropped. I was heartbroken, and—although I wouldn't admit it to myself—I was angry. I'd worked on that speech for almost nine months, putting so much effort into creating a talk that carefully reinforced what the school taught about same-sex relationships. Despite trying so hard to do the right thing, I had been denied.

And I now had to spend the rest of the school year creatively avoiding the question everyone was still asking: "When is your speech at The Gathering? What's the big date, Matthias?"

Maybe this is a sign from God, I thought as the crack inside me grew deeper. *Maybe they really are protecting me from something I don't understand. Maybe this isn't my time to come out yet.*

Since I left the university over a decade ago, I've learned a lot more about how the administration and faculty interacts with LGBTQ+ students, pretending to listen and to offer compassion but refusing to respond when those students are harassed and bullied.

Students, staff, and parents from my university have shared stories of an administration with little room for nuance or understanding. Faculty members who didn't agree with college leaders' rigid beliefs about LGBTQ+ people were strategically weeded out. I was deeply sad, but not shocked, to discover many of the people I turned to for support during my time as a student have since been removed.

Maybe the most upsetting discovery in recent years was that as chair of the Council for Christian Colleges & Universities, the same man who had denied me the opportunity to speak was advocating his fake-listening approach for hundreds of Christian schools across the country.

I know several students at the university have come out in The Gathering since I left. When I talk to current LGBTQ+ students who are out at the school, my sense is that their daily lives are much worse than my closeted experience. The lack of support and compassion extends beyond the administration to the faculty and even to other students.

After I received that email from the chaplain, I took all the work I had put into my speech and hid it in a folder on my computer, wondering if I would ever get the chance to tell the world about who I actually was or if I would stay hidden too.

Warped

When I talk to other runaways, many of them can point to moments like mine, when they were blissfully unaware of what was happening to their faith, but cracks were clearly forming and deepening.

As young people raised in Christianity, it's often easy to ignore critical events with a simple "That's weird. Oh, well, I'll move on with my life" or "Ouch. That hurt. But I'm sure those people in charge know what they're doing."

Again and again, I see runaways like myself who were blind to the larger system, people who could feel the minuscule cracks forming in their faith, even as they believed their faith was getting stronger.

But once those tiny cracks open, it's almost impossible to stop them from getting bigger.

I love a good metaphor, so I like to compare the cracks in my faith, and the faith of other runaways I talk with, to what happened to my floor a couple of years ago.

The building I live in is dug into the side of a hill so that even though it feels like I'm living on the ground floor, in reality I live in a basement.

One morning, I stumbled to my fridge to grab milk for my coffee, and the floor underneath my feet gave a little bounce. Just a slight one as if a bubble had formed underneath the wood, creating a localized mini trampoline.

Strange, I thought as I bounced on it again, trying to smooth it out with my toes. If you haven't noticed yet, I pretty much go with the flow, and my response to most problems is usually, "Meh, it's probably fine. If I ignore it, it will go away." I continued with my day and forgot about it.

A few days later, I was standing at the stove, boiling water, and noticed a bounce in the floor there too. This bubble was bigger. Three of the floorboards were visibly warping, creating what I described to my landlord as a tent—a very bouncy tent. I don't know a lot about carpentry, but I know floorboards aren't supposed to warp and bounce, especially in multiple places.

Throughout the day, the warping increased until the floorboards were almost touching the bottom of my stove, where there was normally a couple-inch gap. I took a photo and sent it off to my landlord, who immediately stated the obvious: "Looks like we might have some water damage."

Carlos, the contractor, came over and confirmed the diagnosis, launching a few weeks of people milling around my place pulling up floorboards, digging outside my window, hosing down walls with water, and making a lot of noise. Carlos explained that the concrete wall by my sink looked like it had cracked, letting moisture trickle in and under the floor, but before they could repair it, they needed to explore how the cracks had gotten there to begin with. They had to figure out what caused the problem; otherwise, it would just happen again.

That's the reality of working with concrete: unless the tension causing it to crack is resolved before repairs, it'll just continue to break again and again.

This truth about one of the most ubiquitous building materials in the world sparked a new understanding about what was happening to me as my faith began to crack under my feet in college.

You can't just treat the symptoms. If you really want to fix something, you must explore the cause, no matter how long or where that exploration takes you.

Pressure

Let's talk more about concrete.

A few months into the coronavirus pandemic, I bought an online class: Concrete Furniture Making for Beginners. It popped up in an Instagram ad, the ones that feel a little bit too targeted.

"Hello, locked-down urban dweller! Here is something just for you. We know about your newfound obsession with concrete. We know."

I had just moved into the previously mentioned apartment, and my favorite thing about it was that it had a massive walk-in concrete shower, bigger than my old bathroom. I told an interior designer friend I wanted to carry concrete through all the rooms as an accent.

"It'll be classy, and concrete is very in right now."

I hit that buy button on the furniture class impulsively. I still had an hour or so before my next client video call, so I sat in my office, notepad ready. Time to learn how to be handy.

";Hola, amigos!"

Well, shit.

The entire course was in Spanish. I don't speak Spanish.

This wasn't my first time watching someone make concrete without really understanding what was happening. As a boy, I had watched my dad make concrete on our farm. He'd have a pile of sand on one side, a stack of cement bags on the other, and the big orange concrete mixer, borrowed from Grandpa, in the middle.

"What's the difference between concrete and cement, Matt?"

"Cement is an ingredient in concrete, but it's not very strong without adding sand and rocks. You can't build strong things out of cement."

He'd nod his head and start shoveling sand into the mixer. "Would you go turn on the hose, buddy?"

The thing about working with concrete is that it sets quickly. After it's mixed, you have to work fast because you only have one chance to get it right. Once it sets, it's set.

"Give me another scoop, bud. Don't get it on your hands."

I would help my dad by shoveling the wet, sludgy mix into a lattice of steel rebar as we made a foundation for a new shed or repaired a walkway. He'd work artfully, almost gracefully, smoothing and shaping the mix until its surface looked like a gray mirror, free from imperfections, just smooth and glossy. Even as a kid, I thought that transformation was a kind of magic.

"Furniture?" Dad chuckled on the phone. He was amused and curious—once again not quite sure what to do with what I was telling him. "Out of concrete?"

"Yes, I'm gonna start with some bookends and then try an end table."

"That's going to be pretty heavy."

"I know, Dad. I'm gonna make molds, so the insides will be hollow, and I'll mix in fiberglass aggregate with the water and cement to make it stronger."

I still think something magical happens when you mix a bit of sand, a bit of cement, and a bit of water. The water begins to react with the cement powder, and it binds together the sand and aggregates mixed in. The moment water is introduced to this mixture, the process of drying and hardening begins, creating what we know as concrete. This happens through a chemical reaction called *hydration*.

This version of hydration is different from what happens when humans drink water to hydrate ourselves. It's tempting to conflate the two, but they're not the same thing.

A scientist would likely disagree with my use of the word *magic* here, but I'm going to stick with it because the Wikipedia article I read about hydration in concrete is far too complicated. I didn't understand a word of it. For example, $2Ca_3SiO_5 + 7H_2O \rightarrow 3CaO \cdot 2SiO_2 \cdot 4H_2O + 3Ca(OH)_2 + 173.6$ kJ.

Let's just agree that it's magic.

Here are two fun facts about concrete:

1. It never stops drying, or curing if you want to sound like you know what you're talking about.
2. If mixed correctly, it gets stronger with age and can even heal itself.

Neat!

Here's another fun fact: concrete has been around since long before what we call the Common Era, in other words, long before Jesus. Before I started working on this book and digging into some research, I didn't know that the Mayans and the Nabataeans used concrete in their structures, some of which are still surviving. The ancient Egyptians and Romans built with concrete too. The aqueducts, the Colosseum, the dome of the Pantheon (which to this day is the largest unreinforced concrete dome in the world) are all made with concrete.

The process of hydration is the reason concrete never stops curing and gets stronger with age. As it cures, it continues to harden—as long as you get the proportions of cement, water, and aggregate correct. Trillions of tiny, microscopic particles within the concrete mixture perpetually react with water, creating chemical bonds through hydration, into infinity.

What does this have to do with our faith?

I'm working on another metaphor. I think we were taught to build the structures of our faith with something very much like concrete.

How many sermons have you heard about building a strong, durable faith? How many books did you get from well-meaning church ladies about strengthening and buttressing that faith because you might lose it in college, even if you were going to a Christian university? How many times did those same church ladies and their husbands warn you that Christianity itself was under attack by Nancy Pelosi and her liberal agenda?

"You're next! She's coming for you next! Is your faith strong enough?"

We were encouraged to craft a faith that continued to harden and strengthen over time. A faith that would be *self-healing* if it ever got damaged.

If you were anything like me as a young person, you knew all the right the Bible verses, the airtight arguments. And if you were lucky, in your backpack you had pseudoscientist Ken Ham's videos explaining that evolution is a conspiracy, ready to hand out to any science teacher who claimed a fossil was millions of years old.

Yes, our parents and church leaders taught us to stick with our faith, to be in the world but not of the world, to be suspicious of everything, to endure "persecution" and laughter. Like many of you, I remember being masochistically inspired by the idea of someone holding a gun to my head just like the story I'd heard about Cassie Bernall, a victim of the school shooting in Columbine, Colorado.

Cassie reportedly was asked by one of the shooters, "Do you believe in God?" as he pointed a gun to her head. When she answered yes, he killed her. This story prompted a flurry of best-selling books, including one by Cassie's mother published only four months after the shooting; hit songs by Christian artists, including Michael W. Smith, Rebecca St. James, and Flyleaf; and countless youth group sermons centered around the idea of martyrdom and the question "Would you say yes?" Christian kids of my generation all prayed we'd be faithful and brave enough to say yes—just like Cassie—to the menacing question "Do you believe in God?"

We imagined ourselves as martyrs for our faith.

As it turned out, the story about Cassie that inspired so many of our church youth groups for years was based on a misunderstanding.[1] The Columbine shooter never asked Cassie that question. Cassie wasn't a martyr. She was simply a victim of a horrific tragedy. Her parents knew mere days after the shooting that their daughter's martyrdom was apocryphal, but they decided to run with the story anyway.

As kids, we didn't know the truth, and our youth pastors used the story and many others like it to teach us that trials of all kinds could be used to strengthen us and, more important, to strengthen our faith.

We vowed we would never become "backsliders." We'd remain faithful through eternity, becoming ever more resilient in the face of adversity—our own version of curing and hydration. And we believed our hardened faith would protect us from life's storms, like all well-built concrete structures do.

We hoped our faith would protect us up until the day we were asked a variation of that fateful question and answered yes. Then we'd have the honor of martyrdom, dying for Jesus, too.

So much pressure. But that was by design.

Compression

If you've ever been to Seattle, you've seen Lake Washington, even if just from the air while flying in. The city of Seattle is squished between the waters of this big lake and the even bigger waters of Puget Sound, which inhibits expanding the infrastructure of the city. On the other side of Lake Washington is another city, Bellevue, and the rest of Washington state.

Every day, on average, about 175,000 cars pass from one side of Lake Washington to the other. Lake Washington is nearly two hundred feet deep, with hundreds more feet of silt covering the floor of the lake. Solid ground is a long way down. And that, according to the experts, makes traditional bridge building nearly impossible. Combine all that silt with the state's propensity for earthquakes, and the fact that Seattleitcs really like unobstructed views of the mountains while boating, and you'll discover why suspension bridges are out of the question.

Engineers had to find another way across the lake, and they did.

I've always been wary of bridges, and the first time I crossed Lake Washington only heightened my phobia. We went through a tunnel and immediately started descending down, down, down toward the bright-blue lake until I-90 seemed to be hovering only a few inches above the water. I had never been on a bridge like this before, with water so close to my window.

I felt as if the massive bridge was floating on the surface of the lake. That idea terrified me.

I found out later that the bridge was, indeed, floating. The two bridges that span Lake Washington are the longest floating bridges in the world. They're engineering marvels, and both are built of—you guessed it—concrete.

As if I wasn't already scared enough of the floating bridges in my backyard, I recently saw an episode of the TV show *Impossible Engineering*[1] in which John Sleavin, senior technical adviser on the Highway 520 bridge project, explained the complexity of designing a floating bridge that both trains and cars can use. If two trains pass by each other (which they do, multiple times a day over Lake Washington), they can generate over seven hundred tons (1.4 million pounds) of weight and pressure, all bearing down on a small portion of the bridge span. And that only accounts for the trains, not the additional hundreds of cars on the bridge at any given moment.

Sure, I thought, let's just throw millions of pounds of steel and people on slabs of concrete floating over very deep, very cold water and see what happens. How could the bridge possibly stay afloat? And how could the concrete stay solid under such immense pressure when the foundation in my little apartment building is full of cracks?

I stared at the TV as Sleavin explained that the answer lies in nearly seventy-eight thousand feet of steel cable in the inner chambers of the bridge. Engineers use hydraulic systems to winch these cables tight in opposite directions, compressing the concrete in the bridge. This reinforces the strength of the bridge significantly and uses a defining principle of concrete to the engineers' advantage: *its density increases under compression*, making it incredibly strong.

Concrete grows stronger when compressed, but the flipside is that when it meets any kind of tension, any force that pushes or pulls on it without compression, it fractures and crumbles almost instantly.

The ratio is roughly 10:1. Concrete can withstand ten times more compression than tension. This makes concrete incredibly durable in some situations but also incredibly brittle in others.

I realized, listening to Sleavin's elegant explanation of elemental forces at work, that he could have been describing my faith—the faith so many in my generation had built our lives on. Ours was a faith strong under pressure but brittle under tension.

Tension

I didn't know how brittle my faith was back in my early twenties. I walked out of college, diploma in hand, more confident than ever that I had a story to tell about God's faithfulness despite what I still believed to be my sinful desires.

I had no clue that a new tension had already been introduced into my life and that this tension, and the possibility my faith could weaken or crumble, was growing stronger.

Pretty soon after graduation, I shared with my mom that I was ready to come out. It wasn't the first time I had mentioned it, but this time I told her I had formulated a plan. The plan seemed simple to me and was born in part because I had rediscovered my childhood love of writing.

I had started blogging in college, and people were even reading my posts. The blog would be the perfect place for my announcement, a way to finally get the weight of this secret off my shoulders and out into the world. I had already written the post, based in part on the speech I hadn't had a chance to give.

Mom gripped her coffee cup a little tighter. "Honey, you know we've talked about this, and your dad isn't fond of the idea of you coming out."

I just looked at her and smiled, giving her time to think. She said she'd have a talk with Dad—again.

I was conflicted after that conversation. I knew my mom wasn't exactly *excited* about the idea of a publicly out son.

Because they were missionaries, their entire livelihood and ministry could be on the line. A gay son didn't provide the best optics for folks who were trying to save souls for the Lord.

As concerned as I was for my parents' feelings and livelihood, something else was rising inside me, from the same place the cracks in my faith were forming, and I had to push forward. Deep in my core, I knew I was living a lie. Nothing felt right as long as that lie persisted. To maintain my own integrity, I had reached a point of no return; I *needed* to tell people.

I tried explaining this need to speak the truth to my Dad, but all he could see were the negative consequences.

"What if you're prohibiting God from working in your life?" he asked me. "What if God wants to heal you, but your desire to identify this way is stopping that work? What if you become straight in the future? What will you do then if you've already come out?"

That didn't seem likely. It was all I could do not to roll my eyes as he spoke, but I stayed silent and waited.

"We can't stop you from posting this, but we want you to be really careful about this decision."

I listened to them list their concerns once more. They were my parents, after all. My dad understood Scripture better than anyone I knew, and I trusted his guidance, even if it seemed to go against my integrity in that moment.

I felt uncomfortable for a long time after that discussion, and I now know that the little hairline fissures in my faith were on the verge of spreading and expanding as the tensions in my life increased.

I kept asking the same questions but arrived at no good answers.

Why didn't anybody in my life want me to be truthful? Wasn't truth one of the highest tenets of our faith? What were they all so afraid of?

Dangerous Virtues

In May 2020, Joe Rigney, president of Bethlehem College and Seminary, the collegiate wing of fundamentalist celebrity pastor John Piper's empire, published a piece titled "Do You Feel My Pain? Empathy, Sympathy, and Dangerous Virtues" in the online magazine *Desiring God*.[1]

This piece served as a follow-up to Rigney's 2019 series on the demonic distortion of compassion, which had thrown people on social media into a frenzy, especially after he published a provocative piece titled "The Enticing Sin of Empathy."[2]

Rigney argued that while compassion, empathy, and sympathy can be good things, they can also cause the person who feels them to abandon "Truth." Invoking C. S. Lewis's narrative format from *The Screwtape Letters*, Rigney's piece includes a series of letters written by imagined demons. If you think Lewis was cheesy, Rigney one-ups him. His character Scratchpot, a dollar-store version of Screwtape, explains to his protégé: "Once untethered from the truth, you'll find that your man is eminently steerable. Things that he would have regarded as foolish, sinful, and ungodly under normal circumstances will sail right under the banner of empathy."[3]

In other words, be very careful, suspicious even, when entering a space where people might be suffering and hurting—your empathy will lead you astray.

Rigney strings together a tightrope of carefully chosen phrases, including making a distinction between "suffering with" and "suffering in" others' pain. He then does his own brand of gymnastics on the tightrope to explain why sympathy, compassion, and empathy are good only up to a point. Past that point—the point of setting aside "truth" for the sake of connection—these virtues become something else.

They become sins.

In Scratchpot's words, "Empathy is a power tool in the hands of the weak and suffering."[4]

A power tool that can destroy walls.

Hot Coffee

Rigney is right, isn't he?

He's correctly diagnosed the main cause of the cracks in the structures that protect us, the walls that hold up our faith. As runaways, each of us can probably point to a moment, or collection of moments, when *empathy*, just simple human empathy, began to crack things open.

A moment when a warm breath of empathy blew through us and we felt a frisson of tension and then saw a pile of rubble in its wake.

My moment happened when I finally finished my coming-out story and hit "share" on Facebook. I had spent most of the night working myself up to posting it, and when I finally did, I swiftly closed my laptop and ran to the bathroom to brush my teeth. All I could think of was that I had to get to bed and close my eyes. I didn't want to face what I imagined all my friends, family, and acquaintances would say about me. I was worried those consequences my dad had warned me about might come true.

Lights off, toothbrush still in my shaking hand, I saw my phone light up.

One notification.

Two.

Three.

Four.

I couldn't look at them. My life had changed in a split second, and I was scared it was for the worse. I was certain all those notifications were from people condemning me, telling me I had abandoned Truth, the church, and God.

I knew I was just beginning to tell the real truth, but that didn't make me any less afraid.

Squeezing my eyes shut and holding on to the edge of the sink, I tapped on one of the message notifications. It was a DM from a professor at my college, one of the smartest people I knew and someone I had long admired. I got ready to feel my stomach drop again, bracing for what I imagined would be the first of many attacks and the start of a long, sleepless night of horror.

"My husband and I just read your post," she said. "We love you deeply and are sending hugs until we can give you one in person. Thank you for having the courage to speak."

My shoulders released a little bit, and I loosened my death grip on the phone. I continued to read messages one by one. All of them were kind—all of them.

That warm breath slid over me, wrapping me in a comfort I hadn't experienced often in my life. It was a feeling of being seen, known for who I was, and loved.

The empathy of all those people reaching out to me with compassion and sympathy pushed on the walls of my faith, introducing new tension. Where I was expecting compression, people trying to convince me I was wrong with forceful words and feeling, I was met with love instead.

It's not that the compression wasn't coming—and swiftly. But that night, the world felt less scary than it had just hours before.

So, Joe Rigney is right. Empathy is a powerful tool in the hands of the hurt and suffering. Whether you're on the direct receiving end, like I was that night, or you feel it move through your body as you see stories of people in pain on film, hear them told in person, or read them in print. Empathy and compassion can shake you to your core, destabilizing your beliefs.

And that can be terrifying.

If you don't push off the feelings of empathy, if you don't immediately run back to dogma to reapply compression to those cracking walls, you start asking more questions.

"Why is this person suffering?"

Even if you do try to reapply compression, reading Bible verses or buying a traditional Christian book on the issue, the cracks will inevitably remain under the surface.

"Why is this injustice happening? Why can't this person's pain be stopped?"

As many runaways I talk to know well, these simple questions are just steps away from bigger, scarier questions about systems of power and privilege. The kinds of questions that might lead people to conclude that too many people are suffering unnecessarily and perhaps the world doesn't have to be this way.

What I've learned since my own walls of faith cracked and crumbled is that empathy, sympathy, and compassion are *forces of human connection* that are hardwired into our very being. We can't escape these forces any more than we can escape gravity.

Empathy, or the experience of feeling the feelings of others, is the result of complex neurobiological processes that we'll explore more later. For now, it's enough to know that our brains and bodies are *designed to be empathetic*. We each have an automatic impulse to reach toward people and help those who are suffering.

We are wired for connection as a way of mitigating pain—our own and others'. For most people, unless this ability to connect is turned away from intentionally and repeatedly, perhaps by fleeing to dogma or rigid definitions of Truth instead of listening to the pain of others, we will continue to experience empathy as a connecting force.

Remember that story about the woman who sued McDonald's because her coffee was too hot? When I was growing up, almost any time someone noticed "Caution: Hot" on a cup, they'd roll their eyes and launch a mini rant.

"Can you believe someone sued McDonald's because their coffee was *hot*? I mean coffee is supposed to be hot, am I right? What an idiot."

In reality, that woman, seventy-nine-year-old Stella Liebeck, had third-degree burns all over her pelvic area because of that coffee.[1] At the time, McDonald's apparently had a policy of keeping its coffee at a resting temperature between 180 and 190 degrees Fahrenheit. It takes a liquid at that temperature just three to seven seconds to cause severe burning if spilled on human skin.

Ms. Liebeck was in the passenger seat of a car, grabbed her coffee, and while the car was still stopped, put it between her legs to add cream and sugar. As she did so, her coffee spilled. It soaked through her pants and onto her inner thighs. Her injuries required skin grafts. This would have been a horrifying injury for anyone, much less a seventy-nine-year-old.

Empathy is what moves us from "What an idiot. Duh, coffee is hot" to "That's awful! I'm so sorry she was hurt" after we hear Ms. Liebeck's whole story.

Even if some of us still think, *Stella really should have known better than to put the coffee between her legs*, we're likely also haunted by the humanness of that action, knowing we've done something similar dozens of times.

If we linger with this story much longer, it's almost inevitable that our next thought expands to the larger systems in place, and we ask some difficult questions: "Why was the coffee that hot to begin with? It really shouldn't be that way. Why wouldn't the company take measures to protect customers from something so clearly dangerous?"

And that was the real reason for Stella Liebeck's lawsuit—to protect other customers from the same fate. McDonald's now keeps its coffee at a lower temperature, for everyone's safety.

Let's return to our concrete metaphor one more time.

The structures of our faith stand strong because of forces I think of as compression, the pressure applied to us to have instant answers to any questions, to be so practiced at apologetics that we as children could win arguments with any "cultic" missionary who came to our doors. Forces of racism, homophobia, sexism, transphobia, ableism . . . the list goes on and on. These forces compressed the walls of our faith, keeping us constantly turning away from anyone we deem different or unworthy.

But sometimes, people get through. When we listen to a friend who is struggling to come out or see a Black man gasping for breath under a policeman's knee, our empathy introduces tension into the walls of our faith. Long, wide cracks might open in one corner or in every one of those walls, and if we're lucky it won't be long before they crumble.

Still Faces

If you've ever taken a psychology course, you've probably run across the still-face experiment. It's brutal, hard to watch.

In this experiment, which originated in 1975, a parent is instructed to interact with their baby normally for a short time. The baby and parent share connection. The baby coos, calls the parent's attention to different things by pointing, and laughs. The parent responds warmly, interacting with the child in a reciprocal way, the way most of us would interact with a baby. Peek-a-boo! All is well.

After about three minutes, the parent is instructed to turn away from their child and then turn back to the child with a completely still face, expressing no emotion and no interaction. Almost immediately, the baby's affect changes from at ease to confused. The baby attempts to get the parent to respond, and as the seconds tick on, their attempts fail, and their distress grows. It doesn't take too much time for the child to start wailing, turning away from the parent, and losing control of their posture. Observers of the experiment see the stress and confusion growing in the baby's tiny body and face.

I tear up almost any time I see videos of this experiment. The baby's panic is difficult to watch as they attempt to get their parent's interaction back. This portion of the experiment only lasts a couple of minutes at most, but those minutes are terrible to endure.

Part of what makes watching so difficult is that many of us know what it feels like to anticipate a warm response from someone only to be met with something completely different. The clammy panic, the racing thoughts. *What's wrong? Something is very wrong. What did I do?*

I felt that panic and anxiety the day after I came out when I got a phone call from a family member. "Your aunt is very upset at you because you didn't warn her about what you posted last night."

I froze, feeling trapped between two responses. Part of me felt guilty; of course, I should've warned her. But another part of me felt incredulous; I didn't owe my aunt a warning. My choice had nothing to do with her! And why wasn't she telling me herself?

I didn't hear a word from my aunt for weeks, which was unusual because we were a pretty close family. Then I got a Christmas card with an ambiguous "let's talk" message neatly printed at the bottom.

We did talk and smoothed over the roughest edges of our relationship, but while we had once been close and communicated frequently, after that incident, we barely ever talked again.

I relate to the baby in the experiment. As I watched my close relationships with many people change after I came out, my distress levels rose. I flailed and squirmed, not understanding why their faces were so still, so emotionless.

At the same time, I started getting messages from strangers who had experiences similar to mine, people who were trying to figure out what to do with their sexuality and their faith. I had no idea there were so many people like me. To my even greater shock, friends started coming out to me on almost a weekly basis.

Virtually all my relationships were changing—some for the worse, many others for the better. And that put me in a confusing place.

When we're faced with a person right in front of us who is in distress, like I was when people started coming out to me, our human instincts beg us to *do something* about that distress. Making the choice to listen and attend to the person is often not difficult, especially if that person is someone we care about.

In the still-face experiment, the moment the parent was allowed to start interacting with their baby again, observers saw and felt the relief of both parent and baby. The parent immediately attuned to their baby's pain, reassuring them that everything was alright.

For many runaways, an initial empathic, human response produced the first hairline fissure in the walls of our faith. The possibility that having empathy or compassion for another person might cause *everything* we believed in to crumble around us didn't even cross our minds.

How could it? We had learned that being a Christian meant weeping with those who weep.

For many of us, things got more difficult when we returned to our faith communities and began to talk about all the little cracks that were forming.

"Look what we've learned since we've been gone. Look at what the Spirit is up to with people on the other side of town and the other side of the world!"

Instead of being met with celebration and warmth, we were met with suspicion, scorn, and contempt.

"How dare you question our beliefs about those people?"

Places that we remembered as full of warmth, community, laughter, and a sense of belonging became cold and silent.

So many still faces.

Our friends and families called us "too compassionate," reminded us to stay close to the Truth, chastised us for walking on dangerous ground.

"Don't give in to sinful desires. Keep your eyes on Jesus!"

The church ladies gave us new Bible verses to meditate on. New ways to compress the walls and keep them standing strong.

But we couldn't forget the people we had seen who were suffering. And often, we were among those people in distress. We were waking up to our own pain.

The cracks grew and grew and grew until we stopped asking, "What is wrong with me?" and began asking, "What is wrong with this community? This church? These people?"

One morning, we woke up to discover that everything we had taken as Truth had crumbled with the walls around us. And the people we thought would always be there for us were gone.

A new, urgent question haunted us as we walked amid the rubble: "Am I even a Christian anymore?"

Reinforcement

I'd like to say that I leaped at the chance to ask big questions, to search for answers about my faith. But in the weeks and months after I came out, I wasn't ready. Met with the still faces of my aunt and a growing collection of confused friends, I decided the best thing I could do would be to help them see my humanity. Maybe I could convince them I was still the same Matthias they knew so well. My being gay didn't have to change anything between us.

I started writing regularly on my blog about what it was like to be gay, celibate, and Christian. I hoped my readers would see that my faith was still as important to me as it had always been.

I was grabbing my little buckets of cement, sand, and water, proving to everyone that I still had what it took to live inside those familiar walls, still had the tools at hand to reinforce them.

But the kindness of so many people in my life at that time kept up the tension pulling at me and my faith every day, demonstrating that I didn't have to stay within those walls or conform to a belief system that caused me pain in order to be loved and cared for.

Remember, empathy invites us outside of our own experience and into the experience of another, which can create tension as it bumps up against our belief systems. At the same time, empathy can also invite us to take our own experiences more seriously, to reconsider what we might have taken for granted, and to see the world with new eyes—acknowledging what's wrong, revealing other truths.

For us runaways who have tried to fit ourselves into concrete boxes of belief, there comes a time when empathy and the struggle we feel inside beg us to acknowledge our own suffering.

When I looked at the world with new eyes, I acknowledged that I didn't *want* to be celibate. I didn't want to be single.

I heard stories of other LGBTQ+ people who believed God was okay with queer relationships. Those stories were scary and alluring. I struggled to understand them.

The walls of our concrete boxes are sturdy, made of heteronormativity, white supremacy, gender hierarchy, ableism, fat phobia—fear of anything "other." And each of us has helped reinforce those walls in order to survive.

When we've seen other people living free, beyond the walls, we've viewed them with both envy and contempt. But eventually, the cracks forming in our walls are impossible to ignore, and we're faced with a quintessential Christian choice:

Do we stop to pay attention to the person on the side of the road, or do we ignore them?

Do we offer bread to the person asking us for food, or do we give them a rock?

Do we hear the words of Jesus and act on them, or do we quickly return to the winch of our belief systems and apply more pressure to our safe concrete boxes, loudly calling those beliefs the Truth, hoping they'll protect us?

Do we retreat into what we used to believe about that person in front of us and about ourselves?

Or do we listen to the person in front of us?

Do we listen to ourselves?

Eventually, I listened. And I found the courage to ask the first of many big questions: Could someone be in a queer relationship and still be a real Christian? Could I?

Part 3

Dirt

Weeds

When I was a kid, in the late summer, people would come from miles around to marvel at my dad's gardens. They'd exclaim about how big the plants were and how much they were producing: purple beans, red and yellow tomatoes, and marbled eggplant. My dad would beam with pride, handing out cherry tomatoes to every person he could find, and I'd race to grab my share. They'd explode on my tongue, the intensity of flavor catching me off-guard, no matter how many I'd eaten.

I can still see Dad dropping the shiny red balls into pint- and quart-size baskets, his hands crusted deep brown with the soil he had worked so hard to cultivate.

His soil.

But I don't want this image to seem too romantic. The gardens came at a cost. We spent hours upon hours upon hours out in the hot sun, watering and weeding.

It was a family affair, with my mom in her giant blue sunhat, rounding us up: "It's time for us to go out and weed!"

Every day, my two sisters and I would venture into the garden to pluck the little green tendrils that weren't supposed to be there, protecting the young vegetables and berries from competition.

As we worked, my mom's thoughts would turn toward the spiritual, as they almost always did—and still do.

"Do you remember the story Jesus told about the soil?"

We were young enough that it was still fun to listen to Mom repeat stories from the Bible, no matter how often we had heard them before.

She'd tell us the parable about the farmer who scattered seeds all around his land. Wildflowers maybe, she embellished, letting us imagine the colors and textures. Wildflower seeds are planted by scattering.

"Those seeds fell in many different places, some on the path nearby, some on rocky ground, some in places where plants were already established, and some on soil."

We'd stop her before she started explaining the difference between soil and dirt for the hundredth time. "We know, Mom, there's a difference."

"Only the seeds that fell on the good, fertile soil grew and produced a field of flowers. The rest of them were plucked up by birds, dehydrated, or choked out by other plants." Mom would explain how all the work we were doing in Dad's garden was creating good soil.

Before composting was cool, we saved all our food remnants and fed them to the worm farms that sat behind the house in giant Rubbermaid containers, worms we later helped incorporate into the gardens. Squirming and squiggly, they were one of the secrets of Dad's amazing yields. So much work, so much intention, went toward creating healthy soil that helped his plants flourish.

"Jesus isn't just talking about gardens here. He's talking about us," Mom continued. We knew that, too, but we'd listen to her unpack the metaphor anyway. The seeds were the gospel; the different types of ground were different types of people.

Somehow, stories about seeds and gardens always got back to sin.

"All humans," she said, "no matter who they are, start off like the first kind of dirt because of sin. Compressed, hard dirt.

Dirt where nothing can grow, where seeds can't even take root. Dirt devoid of nutritional value—or any kind of value."

That may sound harsh to some of you. People devoid of value? Mom was sharing an explanation common in the farming communities of Iowa. Even as kids, we knew this wasn't just about different kinds of soil and people; it was a story that explained the progression of God's work in our lives.

We start off as dirt. If we are lucky enough to hear the gospel and believe it, then the dirt starts to break up a little bit, exposing rocks, becoming a place where maybe seeds can start growing. But it's up to us, and to God, to get rid of the rocks. Slowly, over a lifetime, we must throw out the rocks of doubt and evil, making room for plants of Christian faith to take root. And then we have to weed, getting rid of any competing beliefs, anything that might prevent the gospel from continuing to flourish.

"You know, in heaven, there will be no weeds," my dad would say. The real weeds and rocks in our gardens came from the curse God laid upon the earth because of Adam and Eve's original sin. God put rocks and weeds everywhere to make us work because working was a curse, the result of sin.

I sat cross-legged in the dirt, sweating and pulling up clumps of weeds, listening to my parents tell these stories. I was always seething.

I hate Adam, I thought. *Everything is his fault. I hate him, hate him, hate him.*

Preparation

Several months after I came out in my early twenties, I sat at the small boutique branding agency in Arkansas where I was working. I was a graphic designer, my dream job. Staring at my computer screen, I saw that our chief marketing officer had just updated the agency's Facebook page with a quote of the day: "If you don't like the direction you're going, change it."

Most days, I would have scrolled right by that little nugget of inspiration, but on this day, the meaning hit me in the gut. That morning, I had received an email from an admissions counselor for a graduate school in Seattle informing me that I had to decide immediately whether I would accept or decline their invitation to study for a master's degree. Going to grad school had always been a pipe dream, a plan I thought I'd never be able to follow through on. I had applied to The Seattle School of Theology & Psychology before finishing college, was offered a slot, but deferred when the demands of real life took over, and I took the aforementioned dream job instead.

I didn't tell anybody—even my closest friends—about the deferral or that I couldn't quite let the dream go. In my first few months on the job, I snuck out a few times on my lunch breaks to talk to my admissions counselor in my car, asking every question I could think of. After each call, I'd scold myself and try to forget about what seemed like an unattainable goal.

You can't do this, Matthias. You already made your choice. You're gonna be a graphic designer for the rest of your life.

The email from my admissions counselor was clear: This was my last chance. The deferment wouldn't be offered again, and if I changed my mind later, I'd have to restart the multimonth application process, with no guarantee I'd be accepted a second time.

I sent a brief response, declining the offer and thanking her. She responded with some paperwork to make it official that I was giving up my place.

But when that Facebook quip popped up, I knew immediately that I *didn't* like the direction I was going at all. Although I enjoyed my job, I knew being a graphic designer was not my life's work. On a more personal level, I didn't like explaining to friends and colleagues that I could be gay *and* devoted to my faith and never being taken seriously. By that point, my blog was gaining traction, but as more people read it, I got more messages telling me I didn't know what I was talking about. A lot of commenters said I was twisting the Bible to meet my own desires.

At the same time, I was wading into new territory with my parents, trying to explain that just *maybe* I didn't have to be celibate. They weren't listening. Instead, they suggested getting back into Scripture, studying more, and trusting God to lead me back to the Truth.

After I sent the response to my counselor, I sat motionless as my mind raced. Why had I refused the offer? Why couldn't I move to Seattle? Plenty of people I knew were in grad school, so why not me? An official document—a master's degree in theology and culture—might finally legitimize my ideas and show everyone how seriously I took my faith. Maybe my parents would even stop being suspicious of my challenges and be proud I was getting a deeper theological education.

At the end of the day, I sped home to call one of my sisters and talk through the decision.

"Is this crazy?"

"It's not," she reassured me.

In an adrenaline rush, I printed the paperwork. My hand shook as it hovered over the two checkboxes, "decline admission" and "accept admission." I lowered my pen to the paper and whispered a prayer. I signed my name as quickly as I could and stuffed the paper into an envelope. I ran to the mailbox down the block, dropping the letter into its blue metal prison, ensuring I couldn't fish it out later that night if I changed my mind. I was moving to Seattle.

I called my parents the next day to share the news. They'd been living in Romania doing missionary work for the past several years. I calculated the time difference so it would be midafternoon, before their dinnertime.

"Your dad's out in the gardens working on his soil, and I'm making bread for dinner," my mom announced. I imagined her wiping her hands on her favorite red dish towel after kneading her bread and setting it aside to rest. And I imagined my dad with his tiller, pouring out bags of potassium, nitrogen, compost, and who knows what else. He'd be precisely measuring nutrients and mixing them into the ground, just like he did in Iowa, preparing the ideal environment for seeds and plants. I could still smell the scent of warm earth, damp from melting snow, from the last time I'd visited them.

"It's soil, not dirt," he'd always tell me, the origin of what Mom repeated. "Dirt has no value because it's devoid of nutrients. That's not what we want. We want soil, Matt." Soil teeming with worms and healthy bacteria, its pH balance perfectly tuned to 6.5. Crafted soil.

I filled Mom in on my decision to move to Seattle. There was a lot to catch her up on, admitting that I had only deferred my admission and that I had continued dreaming about grad school for months without telling anyone.

"What about your job? How are you going to pay off your loans?"

I ignored her questions because I didn't want to admit I had no idea how I'd pay off the loans. Instead, I rattled off a few facts about how beautiful Seattle is. "I think it'll be good for me!"

I also didn't want to admit I was hoping to find a community of queer people and maybe even try to start dating. The prospects in my small town in Arkansas hadn't been very good.

My dad got on the phone a few minutes later, and I repeated the highlights. Neither of my parents could understand why I would suddenly give up everything I had spent years working toward to study theology, a pursuit that didn't have very good job prospects for straight folks, let alone someone gay.

I saw their point. I feared the same things they did. Plus, I was still recovering from sticker shock after looking at Seattle apartments online. I'd be paying triple my current rent for a place a quarter the size. With no job and more student loans.

But I knew I had made the right choice.

I was taking a tiller to my life, sure that something new and nourishing would grow.

Seeds

I moved to Seattle a few months later with $400 in my pocket, ready for a new life. Ready to cultivate the soil and let seeds grow. Ready to prove to everybody, once and for all, that I was acceptable just as I was.

In that parable of the farmer who scattered seeds, Jesus asks his listeners to consider that humans are like soil. But within a breath or two, he tells a story in which he compares humans to seeds instead. Seeds that fall in different places and grow.

Instead of thinking of myself as a plot of soil and thinking of my faith (or lack of faith) as a seed that falls and grows within me, I now think of myself as the seed.

I think all of us runaways are seeds with enormous potential to grow and bloom.

In the spring when my dad was tilling the garden back in Iowa, mixing his bags of nutrients into the soil, he would map out different parts of the garden for different vegetables. He'd then mix nutrients in different ways depending on what zone of the garden he was in. A particular combination for each variety.

My dad knew what any good gardener knows: Different seeds require different types of soil, different conditions, and blends of nutrients to create optimal homes. You can't just throw seeds in any old soil and expect them to grow perfectly. The environment is incredibly important.

It's why my dad's tomatoes always tasted better than the tomatoes of any of the ladies from church.

People need the same kind of nourishment and care, the right mix to grow and flourish. We can't just grow anywhere, like within concrete boxes, for example. Seeds—including mustard seeds—can't germinate in concrete. They're likely to get eaten up by the birds, never to be seen again.

Or maybe not.

Birds don't just eat the seeds they find. Some birds— chickadees, for example—grab seeds and fly off to store them for the winter. Chickadees are peculiar as they place each seed they find in a different location, preferring that to a centralized storage place, but somehow remember where most of them are.

But, of course, some seeds are forgotten. Or lost. Or taken by other birds or animals. But the important thing to know is that because of the birds, seeds are able to migrate.

Charles Darwin remarks on this in his seminal work *On the Origin of Species.* A friend of his, Professor Newton, once sent him the leg of a dead bird, as good friends often do. Attached to that leg, Darwin found "a ball of hard earth adhering to it and weighing six and a half ounces."[1] Darwin being Darwin, he took that ball and planted it. That tiny ball of dirt produced eighty-two plants of a variety of different species, causing Darwin to think a lot more about how birds help transfer seeds around the globe.

If we go back to Jesus's parable, I think it's safe to assume that when birds gobbled up the seeds on that hard ground, not all of them were destroyed.

Some of those seeds that fell on the hard path probably wound up somewhere else, maybe in different soil that wasn't so hard. Or rocky. Or weedy. Some must have ended up in soil where they could flourish. The kind of fertile, welcoming places us runaways are looking for.

I don't suggest this alternative to eclipse the metaphor Jesus uses as an example of where our seeds of faith can flourish. It's a beautiful metaphor, and we'll return to it. But I'm now convinced it's incredibly important for us to think of ourselves first not as the soil in the metaphor but as the seeds—maybe even seeds that can migrate.

Rootings

Dr. Angela Parker's heels clicked on the wood floors as she made her way over to one of the lounge chairs she had placed in a corner of her office in the Red Brick Building, our affectionate name for The Seattle School. She was always poised and curious, with the mind of a scholar, but today she was operating in the mode of academic adviser.

"What are you wanting to write about, Matthias?"

It was already time to start thinking about my capstone thesis project for my theology degree. Whatever I chose would help inform my next couple of years of study and help shape my reading list.

"I want to do something exploring a queer theology of relationships."

She nodded.

I explained that I wasn't really interested in trying to defend the possibility of same-sex relationships from a scriptural perspective. That seemed kind of boring to me, and so many people were already doing it. But I was interested in approaching the idea of how God might be folding in and blessing same-sex relationships even though that wasn't part of the original design. I wanted to write something more *constructive* than defensive, I told Dr. Parker.

I sketched out some ideas. I'd start in Genesis, explore God's original design for relationships, how sin messed everything up by introducing other relational options. And I'd try to track how same-sex relationships can still be blessed, grounding that argument in stories of the New Testament. These were early thoughts, but I was proud of them. I even imagined what it would be like to share this completed work with people back home so they could see that I was taking the Bible seriously.

Dr. Parker listened patiently, her face growing more puzzled as I continued to talk.

"Who have you already been reading? Any womanists?"

I shook my head. I barely knew where to start. I told her I hoped she might be able to help guide me. Dr. Parker's own scholarly work was in the womanist tradition. Womanism is a branch of theology that distinguishes itself from white feminism by focusing primarily on Black women's experiences and ideas. She had been making waves in the academic world by combining postcolonial thought and biblical scholarship.

"I love that you're wanting to write about who you are, Matthias. I'm going to give you a list of people to read. But before I do that, I need you to seriously consider your starting assumptions."

I stared at her blankly. "I'm not sure what you mean."

"You're making a pretty big statement there at the beginning. Do you know what it is?"

Searching through everything I had told her, I landed on what I thought she might be getting at. "You mean the original design part?"

Her face confirmed I had understood, but resistance churned in my stomach. She seemed to be asking me to rethink what was so obvious to me: God *originally* intended intimate relationships for only men and women. It was right there in Genesis, wasn't it?

"Are you saying you think same-sex relationships were part of God's original design?"

She smiled, a smile I now recognize on my own face when people ask me a question about theology that reveals we're living and thinking in entirely different worlds.

"I'm asking you to consider what you're rooting your project in. Why do you think you are trying to build something from a theology of shame?"

Her question took me by surprise in the moment and has stuck with me for all the years since that meeting. At the time, my mind couldn't conceptualize what she meant. The Bible was about God's original design for humanity. That seemed indisputable. My desire to be in a relationship with a man didn't meet that ideal, but it was also obvious to me that my sexual orientation wasn't something I chose, so surely God had also made provisions for people like me. That's all I wanted to explore—how God's grace could make a way forward for people who cannot meet a biblical ideal.

How were my ideas *shame-based?* Did Dr. Parker think gay people existed before sin entered the world?

I fidgeted in my seat, and my mind wandered to what another professor had said in a recent class. One of the psychology professors at the school, Dr. O'Donnell Day, occasionally shared what she called "ordinary thoughts." These were her attempts to bridge the worlds of psychology and theology. She never spoke in a cringey everything-has-to-be-linked-back-to-the-Bible "Christian therapy" kind of way. Her reflections on big spiritual questions were based on years as a psychologist who practices analytically.

She insists everyone call her "O'Donnell," not "Dr. Day," so I'll oblige her here.

O'Donnell always started with the same caveat: "Now, I am not a theologian . . ." which made me laugh and shake my head. I became convinced pretty quickly, after only hearing her speak once or twice, that she was one of the best theologians I'd ever known.

In a latent southern drawl, she shook her bright white curly hair and returned again and again to a key concept, making sure we understood her well: "Your theology is only as good as your psychology."

"Your theology is only as good as your psychology."

Both Dr. Parker and O'Donnell were getting at something I didn't yet understand, but sitting in Dr. Parker's office that day, I knew I wanted and needed to understand. At that time, I didn't think of myself as especially ashamed. I wasn't driven by shame at all, quite the opposite. I had read Brené Brown, and I was being vulnerable, wasn't I?

But my professors' words were sticking, seeping into the cracks, and expanding.

Nutrients

Despite all the ways I had begun questioning my theological rootings in my first few months of grad school, I still had a lingering belief that somehow theology is passed down from God to humans in some mystical way that bypasses the human mind. I didn't believe human psychology had *nothing* to do with theology, but I thought theology sort of averages itself out, like a pendulum that eventually stops in the middle. Extreme versions of theology, informed by extremes of human culture, are eventually smoothed out simply by virtue of being passed through the sieve of many generations.

I thought the best parts of any theology would linger, and the worst parts eventually would be relegated to history. Yes, this was an optimistic view, and O'Donnell's perspective soon invited me to challenge it.

To me, it's now obvious that different people are drawn to different understandings of theology, but growing up, I would've told you there was only *one correct theology*—ours—and everything else was sinful placation. I didn't have language to talk about why people understood theology differently, but now I think a helpful way of understanding the whys is to look at environments that shape people.

If we grow up with parents who criticize, a God who criticizes us will sync with our parents' teachings *and* will also feel comforting in a somewhat masochistic way because it helps to regulate our nervous system. Criticism is what we know and understand. It's in our comfort zone.

If we grow up in a family where shame is the primary motivator, we're more likely to find ourselves drawn to a theological system based on shame. Any other way of framing God isn't going to make sense to us because it's outside our context, outside our modes of understanding. A shame-based theology will reinforce our understanding of the world *and* will also alleviate some of our pain. In a shame-based theology, we strive for perfection in this life with the assurance that perfection will eventually come when we're dead.

As a young grad student, I thought I understood the power of environment to shape theology, but Dr. Parker invited me to consider it more deeply. She asked me to look at my own theological dirt, so to speak, to examine where I was planted, and to discover what nutrients made up that soil, if any. What role did shame play in my environment?

In the years since that conversation in Dr. Parker's office, I've gained more language to describe the environments in which runaways are planted and how they grow and thrive despite harsh conditions. Many of us landed in rocky soil, maybe in weedy soil. Some of us were stuck for years on the hard path where nothing grows.

If we were lucky, even those harsh environments allowed us to germinate. We got enough nutrients that we could peek our little leaves out of the ground and feel the warmth of the sun. We got a taste of home and comfort, but that home eventually became stifling.

I think of a fern outside my living room window, growing on a nearby terrace. For the life of me, I can't figure out how it is still alive, growing in a rocky corner where it gets barely any light and no water at all because it's completely covered from any rainfall by the decks above it.

That fern is withered and stunted but continues to grow, adding fronds and shivering in the breeze.

If I were a motivational speaker or a pastor, I might say that fern demonstrates that life can grow anywhere. I might try to inspire you to *grow where you are planted*. If that little fern can survive, you can too. Keep going! Endure!

But I know the stories of so many runaways whose religious environments withered and stunted them and nearly destroyed them. They grew, sure, but they didn't thrive. And it would be cruel for me to tell those people to keep going and endure, to pump them up and tell them to wait patiently for some future when all ferns get enough water and warmth—especially if I know there is better soil, a better environment just around the corner.

Even crueler would be for me to blame the runaways for their lack of growth. "Hey, little fern, keep reaching deeper for nutrients. Keep thinking about the rains that will eventually blow in. The only thing holding you back is yourself!" Of course, that's nonsense.

Isn't that the same as someone telling us runaways that the only thing holding us back from flourishing is not reading the Bible enough, not praying enough, or not prostrating ourselves on the floor enough?

The problem for the fern is that it doesn't have enough nutrients or water, and no amount of encouragement will change that. Likewise, to encourage someone to root themselves deeper to find the Living Water masks the true problem.

In the case of the runaway seeking home and comfort and truth, the true problem takes us back to Dr. Parker's initial question: Have we rooted our lives in a theology of shame?

Fertilizer

I've learned a whole lot more about shame since those conversations with Dr. Parker and O'Donnell. And while I've uncovered the ways that shame harms and holds us back, I've also uncovered the ways that shame can motivate. People look at me funny sometimes when I suggest that shame has motivational properties. I think it's because many of us are used to hearing about all the ways shame shuts us down. Initially, it can be hard to imagine how something that makes us feel so small and incapable can be an extremely powerful tool to move us toward action. But once I start talking about it, the idea seems to click for people pretty quickly.

One of the ways I understand shame is as the identity-construing messages we adopt about ourselves. Guilt is the feeling that "I've done something wrong/bad/I'm not proud of." Shame is a message we get that tells us, "I *am* something wrong/bad/I'm not proud of."[1] That message hits us at our core, makes us believe it's who we are.

The voice of shame tells us *we are the bad thing we are most scared of.*

When we're stuck in shame, we believe there's no use trying to do anything about it because it's the way things will always be.

Unless, of course, there's a possibility things can get *worse.*

When things getting worse is on the table, we move from being stuck in how awful we are to a laser focus on not devolving the situation. If we believe we're the ones who got ourselves into whatever mess we're in, then it's also our responsibility to make sure we don't muck it all up even more.

If someone taps into my fear that things might get worse, they have a powerful recipe for motivating me. Many of us know this intuitively because of all the ways we motivate ourselves. We fear that if we're not hard on ourselves, we'll turn into lazy good-for-nothing slobs.

Dr. Kristin Neff is a compassion researcher who writes extensively about shame. Neff says we all "cling to this approach with ourselves, believing that self-flagellation (even if only mental) is both useful and effective. It's the old carrot-and-stick approach—self-judgment is the stick, and self-esteem is the carrot. If you do what you're supposed to do even though you don't want to, you can avoid being bashed with self-criticism and feel better about yourself."[2]

After you start to see shame as motivation, it's hard not to see it almost everywhere. It can be as blatant as an Olympic coach berating a player in front of the world or far subtler. And as a mentor of mine, Dr. Dan Allender, often says, "The more subtle, the more insidious."

When we're swimming in the waters of shame as motivation, especially when it's subtle, it's difficult to notice how shame is affecting us. It's easier to spend our time striving to make our lives better or trying to mold ourselves into the kind of people we think Jesus wants us to be instead of slowing down and recognizing the shame.

In my first book, *Beyond Shame*, I talk about a coping mechanism we use to work with shame called *shamefulness*. Shame as motivation is a classic example of being *in shamefulness*. Paradoxically, we heap more shame upon our shame in order to keep ourselves from feeling shame.

Dr. Neff describes how this approach "only [works] for one reason: *fear*. Because it is so unpleasant to be harshly criticized by ourselves when we fail, we become motivated by the desire to escape our own self-judgment. It's like we're putting our own heads on the chopping block, constantly threatening the worst, knowing that the terror of our own harsh self-criticism will prevent us from being complacent."[3]

If our self-judgment is paired with threats of external judgment, these feelings become even stronger. If that external judgment is threatened by the God of the Universe, we have a self-reinforcing system.

In that kind of system, we say things like "Jesus, less of me, more of you," thinking we're striving after godliness, while not realizing that within that sentiment is the shame and fear of being *me*.

As if God wants us to become less of ourselves in order to be holy. Does that seem ridiculous?

That's precisely what a lot of Christian theology teaches. That we need to be *less*.

Almost the entirety of the popular Christian understanding of Jesus's work in the world, what folks call the "gospel," or the supposed "good news," is thinly veiled shame. To be honest, a lot of this brand of shame is not veiled at all. When this perspective is all we know, we call it a "Christian worldview."

No wonder we're struggling to grow. We've been planted in soil fertilized with shame.

Bloom

I wish I could tell you that all we runaways need to do to flourish again is to find different soil. If only it were that easy. If only we were just like seeds plucked up from the hard ground by some birds and dropped to a new location, fertile and sweet, just waiting to give us all the warmth and nutrition we need.

All we'd need to do is put down roots, turn toward the sun, and bloom.

We've heard the same advice:

"Just go to a different church."

"Well, not all Christians are like that. You just haven't found the right community."

"Don't give up on God just because some of his people hurt you."

"People will fail you, but God never will."

We've all tried to follow that advice. We've looked for new churches, given people the benefit of the doubt, and tried to cling to a separation between God and humans. But I imagine that since you're reading this book, those things didn't really work for you any better than they did for me when I tried them before entering The Seattle School.

When I first moved to the city, I had heard rumors that there was a big evangelical church in Seattle that had just changed its policy on LGBTQ+ people, becoming fully affirming of queer relationships and even allowing queer folks in leadership—something unheard of in the evangelical churches I grew up in.

That's perfect, I thought. *I'll just go to church there.* It would feel familiar, but I wouldn't have to be scared about being found out. I could just be me.

I walked in one Sunday morning, with a couple of new friends and Bible in hand. The lights dimmed, and the worship band started singing a familiar song. I didn't join in singing; my heart was beating too fast. I looked around at all the faces in the crowd, people singing with their arms raised: *Spirit lead me where my trust is without borders.*

I felt hot, and my throat was dry. I didn't want to be there. Something didn't feel right. But I willed myself to stay in my chair.

Throughout the rest of the service, I kept looking around the room. I knew they said they were accepting LGBTQ+ people, but my body was telling me something different. I didn't feel safe. I kept expecting someone to clock me as gay, pull me aside, and begin to explain to me why I couldn't be a Christian. The Facebook messages I kept getting from "concerned" family and friends would suddenly be personified.

I made it through the service, telling myself, *You're safe here. You're safe here.*

But I didn't *feel* safe. I didn't want to be in church.

Acclimation

Let's talk about plants again for a moment. We'll return to that uncomfortable church and the topic of shame soon.

I don't know if you've ever bought plants from a greenhouse to bring back to your garden, but any plant grown from seed in a greenhouse must be handled carefully before it can begin to thrive in a new home. If you move a plant directly from a greenhouse to your backyard, it will probably die.

It can take a week, sometimes longer, to prepare greenhouse plants for life in the big real world of your garden. For the first few days, you're supposed to leave the plants outside in a place where they don't get direct sunlight, sheltered from any sort of breeze. Let them sit and acclimate to temperature changes. Slowly start introducing direct sunlight, a breeze, maybe some rain. Day by day, expose your little plants to more of the elements, helping them learn to cope with how incredibly intense life outside in the wild is.

It's a slow, annoying process if you're as impatient as I am. I just want to go to the store, put my sunhat and gloves on, and pretend to be the Barefoot Contessa in her garden for an afternoon. Instant, glamorous, master gardener!

Not a chance. No matter how healthy your little plants look, they're not strong enough to face the real world. Your backyard will ultimately, hopefully, be a healthy place for them, but in the short term, there's just too much burning sun, too severe temperature changes, too many new sensations.

If we approach our search for a new spiritual home expecting we will be able to jump into any new environment and thrive, we are as doomed as those little plants. We'll end up burnt and withered, dying despite an apparently nurturing environment all around us.

Frustrating, right?

Like those greenhouse plants, we need time to adjust when moving from place to place, especially if we're moving homes. This is true whether we're talking metaphorically or we're literally moving to a new city. Moving homes, making a big transition, takes time to get used to.

My family moved often when I was growing up, and in those difficult, awkward, lonely times of transition, it was easy to fall into shame-fueled despair.

"Nobody likes me, Mom. What's wrong with me? Why don't I have any friends?"

She'd gently wipe my face and say, "Honey, don't believe those lies you're telling yourself about yourself. We've only lived here six months; it takes two years for a new home to feel like home."

I've clung to that metric in my adult life, and it has mostly held up. Though, in my experience, I think my mom was being generous. Sometimes it takes far longer than two years for a new city to feel like home, even if we are doing everything "right" when it comes to making friends and finding community.

It can take even more time to feel at home when we've left our previous home in a traumatic way—if we've been forced out, or there's been a massive relationship rupture, or if we've finally mustered the energy to *get out* because we know we can't survive any longer.

That's often the definition of us runaways—people leaving home in a traumatic way, knowing we can't survive a minute longer.

Windows

The reason traumas make it more difficult to find home is all about our nervous systems.

In case you didn't memorize your middle-school science textbook, here's a little refresher: Our nervous systems are responsible for essentially everything we feel, think, say, or do. Our five senses are part of the nervous system, and so are our heartbeats and blood flow. The nervous system regulates all the things we do without having to think about them, like reflexes, blinking, breathing, balance, and so on.

That word, *regulates*, is important here because one of the primary functions of our autonomic nervous system (ANS), which controls involuntary processes, is to help regulate our relationship to our environment. This includes not just our physical environment, like our body's response to temperature or threats, but also our emotional environments. At a high level, our ANS essentially attempts to keep us in a state of balance and harmony wherever we find ourselves.[1]

If a threat appears, our ANS goes into overdrive, prompting us to fight or flee before we're even consciously aware of the threat. Sometimes it shuts us down, leading us to feel numb or frozen. Other times, we may stop thinking and become incredibly compliant in order to mitigate the threat. In doing all this, the goal is survival. Our ANS seeks to return us to a nonthreatening place and reestablish equilibrium.

These responses are often referred to as the *fight-flight-freeze-fawn* phenomena, and they're paired with what psychiatrist Dr. Dan Siegel calls our "window of tolerance." This window is the space in which our nervous systems operate successfully and maintain and regulate our relationship with the environment.[2] When we're outside our window of tolerance, we're *dysregulated*, slipping into a survival mechanism. (The survival options are, as you'd expect, fight, flight, freeze, or fawn.)

Dr. Siegel's ideas about the window of tolerance help me explain the nervous system to my clients in therapy. When we're in our window of tolerance, I tell them, we feel we can handle what life throws at us. If something difficult happens, we may feel a bit flustered or raw, but ultimately it doesn't faze us too much. We're able to be present with ourselves and others.

It's important to note that being in the window of tolerance doesn't mean we necessarily feel happy, at ease, and at peace. We may feel anxious, or depressed, or any number of things while within the window. However, those feelings don't overwhelm us; they're not too much for us to handle. They don't push us over the edge into dysregulation.

At the upper end of the window of tolerance is what Dr. Siegel calls *hyperarousal*—the fight and flight responses. When we're hyperaroused, our bodies are preparing to do battle or flee. Our sympathetic nervous system takes over, elevating us. We may feel incredibly anxious, full of rage, emotionally flooded, or, on the extreme end, have panic attacks or difficulty breathing. If we've crossed over the line from our window of tolerance into hyperarousal, these things will feel involuntary, uncontrollable. We may not understand why we do the things we do, why we suddenly start crying or feel our heart beating so fast we're afraid something is seriously wrong with our body. Because these responses are beyond our conscious control, we get frustrated and scared.

On the lower end of the window, we slide into *hypoarousal*—our freeze and fawn responses. This is when our parasympathetic nervous system takes over, trying to calm us down. When we're hypoaroused, we may feel shut down, flat, or empty. We may be unable to move, suddenly faint or go to sleep, or move into a dissociative state. Again, these responses are outside our control; they just happen.

The freeze response may be more familiar to you than the *fawn response*, a fourth response to threat that trauma researchers have recently identified and named.

In the fawn response, we become as compliant as possible to avoid real or perceived threats. Think, for example, of when dogs roll over in submission when they get in trouble. This can happen physically but also emotionally. We might lose all sense of our own desires, wants, or needs and almost morph into another person, doing whatever that person wants or needs us to do, as a way of protecting ourselves. This is a form of hypoarousal as well. We calm down the threat with our very bodies.

Here's where things start to get a bit complicated: We aren't born with some innate, standard window of tolerance. In fact, every person's window is a bit different. No two people, when faced with the same stimuli, are going to respond in the exact same way. Some people have extremely wide windows of tolerance, and not much pushes them into a threat response. Other folks have extremely narrow windows, and it seems almost anything can send them into a panic attack or freeze response.

It gets even more complicated because our windows can also change throughout any given day. If we're feeling hungry—you guessed it—our windows shrink.

Ever heard someone say, "Oh, I'm just getting *hangry*." Yup, that's a window of tolerance thing.

Our nervous system isn't able to regulate as well when we're hungry, or sleepy, or distracted, or faced with big-scale threats of war, pandemics, or fill in the blanks. Each of these things can cause our window of tolerance to shrink, and we might go around saying, "I don't feel like myself today" or "Why can't I do as much as I used to? Why am I so tired all the time?"

Complicating factors aside, our windows grow in direct relationship to the worlds we live in. That's another way of saying we each have our own specific window of tolerance that was formed out of our particular context—those environments in which we grow or shrivel up—the ones we've been talking about throughout this chapter.

And because our windows grow in relationship to the specific environments we're in, it makes changing environments that much harder.

In her book *The Wisdom of Your Body*, trauma therapist Dr. Hillary McBride goes beyond the fight-flight-freeze-fawn paradigm to discuss the way our nervous systems adjust to any environment we are in, including environments where we're not safe. If this happens repeatedly, over an extended period, in spaces where we can find little rest or relief, we experience *complex trauma*. McBride writes, "In complex trauma, unrest might actually feel like the easiest, most comfortable place to us. What should feel safe can feel dangerous, and what should feel dangerous can feel safe. It often means that we never learned it was safe to trust, which leaves us feeling desperately alone inside without knowing how to be connected."[3]

Here's the kicker, the part that McBride describes so well: "If this happened at a young enough age, that overwhelm was managed by a shutdown state of shame, the fundamental sense of being 'broken.'"[4]

Thus, the sense of being broken *becomes what regulates us*. Wow.

Some of us, particularly because we lived in religious communities of various kinds, were told we *should* see ourselves as fundamentally broken. We *are* broken, they told us. We arrive in the world *worthless*, already tainted and dirtied by sin as newborns. Feeling broken is normal, good even, because it's the Truth. The only thing that can mend our feeling of brokenness and make life better is to acknowledge our need for a divine savior.

In other words, our brokenness points us directly to God.

One of the ways Dr. McBride defines spiritual trauma is "someone handing you an inner critic and telling you it's the voice of God."[5]

That resonates for me. How about you?

For many of us, the voice of shame *is* the voice of God, or maybe we'd call it the voice of conviction. We're experiencing a combination of complex trauma and spiritual trauma, and those voices don't disappear easily.

When we try to reeducate our nervous systems, which learned how to regulate our bodies within a specific context, to operate in a different context it's rarely going to feel right.

Even if that system is healthier for us, it's not what we're used to, so it's not going to give our bodies comfort. We learned comfort, or some version of comfort, in a different environment, and that doesn't automatically transfer to our next environment.

In practical terms, if you've been sleeping on a shitty mattress for most of your adult life and finally save up enough money to buy a good mattress, that good, supportive mattress isn't automatically going to feel amazing. In fact, it'll probably hurt, make you feel stiff, and even make you wonder if you should have kept the old mattress all along. It's gonna take some sleepless nights and back pain to get used to. Your body is going to sound the alarm: "This is not right. This hurts! Stop!"

Your situation will be confusing because you won't be able to tell which pain is the kind of pain you're supposed to listen to and which pain is just your body getting used to the new thing. You'll be tempted every night to pull out the old mattress.

(Because, of course, you didn't pay the extra hundred dollars to have it removed by the delivery guys.)

When we're running away from an old environment, searching for a new home, it's wise to expect that our new home isn't going to feel comfortable or right initially. Like those little greenhouse plants, we need to acclimate.

Eventually, the new mattress will start to feel good. Comfy even. One night, when a friend from out of town visits, you will generously give up your bed and pull out the old mattress. (No, you still haven't disposed of it after six months because how do you get rid of a mattress? No one knows.)

Anticipating the warm embrace of cheap memory foam, you sink in, expecting pure comfort. You're met instead with a body-shaped canyon that's so deep you can barely get out.

"How did I ever think this was comfortable?"

You're wide awake at 3:00 a.m., doing a reality check. You haven't noticed any lower back pain in months. Your new mattress is comfortable and has changed your quality of life for the better.

Moving environments doesn't mean you might not lie in bed a few years later, listening to doubting voices in your head and wondering if you made the right choice. The same thing will happen in our new spiritual environments. We'll second-guess ourselves:

"Am I ignoring the voice of God to satisfy my own selfish desires?"

"Is this the right resting place for me or another mistake?"

"Have I done everything wrong since running away?"

Lizards

I couldn't have told you this when I was sitting in that chair in a new church, willing myself to stay in place instead of running out the door.

I couldn't have told you this while I was wrestling with the words of Dr. Parker and O'Donnell, trying to understand.

What I now know and can tell you is that in those moments I was waking up to my own complex trauma, the trauma of being shaped and formed in an environment that depended on me seeing myself as fundamentally broken, as fundamentally evil. An environment of shame.

From my experiences at college while trying to come out, and after my move to Seattle put enough distance between my old environment and me that I gained a valuable new perspective, I could see some of the outlines of the shame permeating that old environment. But it took many conversations and a long search for a new church before I could truly see what was going on.

Trauma therapist Resmaa Menakem describes how our nervous systems are connected to what he calls the "lizard" part of our brains as opposed to the "thinking" part. He writes, "All our sensory input has to pass through the reptilian part of our brain before it even reaches the cortex, where we think and reason."[1] He further illustrates: "Many of us picture our thinking brain as a tiny CEO in our head who makes important executive decisions. But this metaphor is misguided: Our cortex doesn't get the opportunity to have a thought about any piece of sensory input unless our lizard brain lets it through. And in making its decision, our reptilian brain always asks the same question: *Is this dangerous or safe?*"[2]

This is vital information for us runaways. The contest between lizard brain and thinking brain helps us put language around the ways we involuntarily react in a variety of situations. As we experience cracks in our concrete walls of faith, as we let empathy in, as we start to wake up to our own and others' experiences of pain, as we ask big questions and start finding some answers, if we're lucky it all begins to connect us to our bodies. Often, for the first time.

Unlike the time I sat in that cathedral pew hearing people cheer for my loneliness, as I sat in that chair in the Seattle church, I was able to connect with myself enough to admit something I had never admitted before: *I don't feel safe.*

Instead of regulating my emotions and physical sensations by telling myself I was fundamentally broken, I let my lizard brain speak to me on full volume and tell my body what I'm sure it had been telling me for most of my life, even though I'd refused to listen. Something that came to my ten-year-old self so naturally.

The lizard brain said just one word: *RUN.*

Part 4

Mirrors

Done

There were no cheese sticks when I ran this time, no carefully packed bags stuffed full of underwear. As I walked out the door of the large brick church and onto the tree-lined sidewalks of one of Seattle's old neighborhoods that autumn morning, my heart was beating fast. Part of me surely knew I wouldn't be returning. Not just to that church but to church in general. I was done.

If even the spaces that explicitly affirmed my belonging felt unsafe—spaces that made room for my whole self as a gay man—if in those spaces I still constantly looked over my shoulder for a catch, I had better ways to spend my Sunday mornings. There were brunches to attend. With mimosas.

I had made a shift from "there's something wrong with me" to "there's something wrong with them" and was on my way to "not just them but this entire system." Up until that point, the compression protecting my once-strong concrete box of belief from crumbling further was my theory that I just hadn't found the right new church yet. Now that wasn't working anymore. My belief had crumbled from all the tension the past several years had introduced—the tension of seeing others' pain first-hand, seeing just how many people were like me, bleeding from the weight of carrying a lifetime of shame-fueled theology. And the tension of watching so much injustice perpetuated by the very people who declared, "This is God's will."

I was fine. Better even. I wasn't hiding anymore, trying to squeeze myself into the sharp and rigid corners of that box. It was like stretching after a long car ride, finally with enough space to expand, grow, and say out loud, "I'm really sore."

The initial feeling I had experienced walking out of that church was not unlike those first thirty minutes or so in the grain bin I ran to as a kid or those runaway games I used to play with my friends in the woods, finding moss and sticks to create a comfortable bed. *Look at me*, I thought. *I can survive out here myself. I'm an explorer, and I can thrive!*

But as metaphorical day turned to metaphorical night, I found myself looking back toward the place from which I came, not wanting to go back but needing the comfort it had once provided.

It was an odd feeling. I knew if I ran back toward my old life and started searching for a church yet again, it wouldn't actually bring any comfort. I was no longer interested in finding the "right" church; I knew that much. There was more turmoil within me than a simple change of location could fix. But at that point in my life, churches were the only form of comfort I really knew.

I began to realize, though, that the kind of comfort I was getting from church was similar to that of a Munchausen-by-proxy patient. Were my church communities hugging me as they slipped rat poison into my food and concocted fake diagnoses? Were they telling me they were nourishing me with Living Water as they ladled bacteria-infested sludge into my mouth? They kept whispering in my ear, assuring me they were the only ones who could give me what I needed. Were they right? It seemed the world in which I had learned to survive for twenty-four years was gone.

I also knew I still wanted to believe in something; I still had a feeling in my body that there was *more* and that maybe I could call that more *God*. Was it all my imagination? I asked myself that every day. I wondered if the only thing keeping me stuck in limbo was an inexplicable desire to believe in more.

Then there was the fear.

When I was fifteen, I sat in a coffee shop with a mentor who drew a spiral on a sheet of paper, telling me it represented my descent into death if I kept following the path of sin I was on. He said that because I already had the power of Jesus within me, all I had to do was turn around and walk up the spiral instead of continuing downward into death. *Just turn around.*

And if I didn't turn around?

God would give me over to my own sin, my mentor told me. If I resisted God's voice too long, it would be too late. Like the story of Adam and Eve in the garden, if I didn't blindly obey the church's rules, God's rules, God would curse and banish me forever. My own disobedience, my own defiance would seal my fate.

Late at night as a kid, I often plugged my headphones into the little portable radio I kept in my room, hiding under the covers and tuning it to Moody Radio, a station run by the Moody Bible Institute, a fundamentalist Christian ministry. I always felt so sneaky listening to the "after dark" programs— the juicy stuff—they'd put on after kids went to bed.

One program was simply testimonies, stories of how people got saved, how they ended up becoming Christians, and it was my favorite. Even at eleven or twelve years old, I loved hearing the dramatized versions of all the bad things people had done before they saw the light. I was enthralled by a world I had never known—drugs, sex, alcohol, prison. One guy became a Christian because he couldn't get hard anymore while having multiple affairs with multiple women. Someone had told him about Jesus, and suddenly he was plagued with erectile dysfunction. No matter what he tried, he couldn't have sex. The only solution, it seemed, was faith in Jesus as his savior and monogamy.

With each story, the background music would swell, people would speak more and more slowly, emotion building in their voices, and they'd share how after accepting Jesus, their lives changed completely. They were miraculously cured of addictions or delivered from mental illness. That guy could get hard again but only with the woman he married. Praise the Lord.

I don't doubt that many of these people did experience life changes, nor do I doubt their stories were true. There are many mysteries in this world. But these stories, and their counterparts told in churches and at summer camps throughout my life, set me up for hundreds of nights spent in anguish. For the people on the radio, Jesus was magical—or, to use the Christian term, *miraculous*. They lived in defiance of God's truth but eventually reached a breaking point when they confessed all their sins, and just like that, they were cured. They didn't have to struggle with those sinful desires anymore.

From defiance to compliance. Amen.

But it didn't work like that for me. When the testimonials ended, I turned off the radio, and my thoughts wandered. I thought maybe I could try to help that guy get hard myself. Then I'd flush with shame, confess, apologize to God, and go to sleep.

As a therapist and as a podcaster, I've listened to so many people who have their own version of my story. If God could miraculously save all those *really* "bad people" from all their desires, what did it mean when God didn't choose to deliver some of *us*? Maybe we weren't trying hard enough? Maybe we hadn't hit rock bottom? Or maybe we didn't want salvation enough? Maybe we'd have to learn the hard way.

As I thought about my exit from the church and what might come next, I wondered if I was about to learn the hard way.

Desire

By the time I was twenty-four, I wasn't regulating myself by feeling fundamentally broken anymore. But I was still suspicious of myself. I was running away but not fast enough to outpace the lingering tendrils of shame.

All I had taken for granted about my faith up until that point was being shaken as I sat in classes and had conversations in the halls of The Seattle School. The head of the theology department, Dr. Chelle Stearns, often pulled out her beloved violin, which she called Danny, to accompany her lectures. One day, she began with an exclamation:

> Today we're talking about Augustine, desire, and music! Rowan Williams, in his book *The Wound of Knowledge*, talks about Augustine in such a way that *desire is the very thing that leads us into God.* And that the spiritual life is, in some ways, asking the question: What do we do with unmet desire? How do we actually live with unmet desire in our lives? How do I, how do *we*, identify desire and how it's awoken in us? And how do we deal with unmet desire that then meets us in the process of our desires awakening?[1]

She taught in a circular way that kept me dizzy, each point punctuated by her playing on her violin. She invited us to *feel* theology, *feel* desire, *feel* the movement of energy that happens in a room whenever music is played.

This was a vastly different way of understanding God than I had ever encountered, an approach that didn't seem to be pressing on my wounds but instead sparked my imagination. I turned her ideas over in my head: Desire might be the very thing that leads us into God? What could that mean? Desire was something to be saved from, scrubbed clean from, wasn't it? Desire led us completely away from God and into sin.

In my world, *desire* always meant something sexual; it was a code word for *fleshly desires*, which meant *dirty desire*, which meant *sex*. It was something to stay away from, unless, of course, you were married. And even then, you had to keep it in check.

Bottom line: *Desire* certainly didn't mean anything good. The only way desire could be good was if we paired it with God. *Godly desire*, that was the good kind of desire. Humans were incapable of good desire on our own; we had to have God's help. And even with God on board, our desire was dubious unless we could back it up with a Scripture reference or two—or seven.

I posed a question to Chelle in the hallway one day after her lecture on desire: "When you say desire can lead us into God, you don't mean sexual desire, right?"

I saw the same smile I had seen on Dr. Parker's face. "Why wouldn't I? Sexual desire is a form of desire, isn't it?"

I quickly nodded and walked away. I had to sit with that answer for a while.

Eventually I realized that instead of meaning *wanting a bad thing*, Chelle defined desire as more akin to the simple word *want*. For example, "I desire that ice cream" is the same as "I want that ice cream."

The word *want* doesn't quite capture the full meaning of desire because it's a little bit too glib, a bit too on the surface. Desire is fuller, more complete, deeper than want. It's something that flows out of who we are as people, our human natures. What I struggled to understand was that for most of the professors at The Seattle School, desire was fundamentally seen as *good* precisely because it's part of what makes us human.

Months after listening to Dr. Stearns's first discussion of desire, I was reading theologian Sarah Coakley's book *God, Sexuality, and the Self.* She writes about desire as "the precious clue that ever tugs at the heart, reminding the human soul— however dimly—of its created source."[2] She continues, "Desire is an ontological category belonging primarily to God, and only secondarily to humans, as a token of their createdness 'in the image.'"[3]

If you're like me and have to google the word *ontological* every time you see it, let me save you the trouble. Ontology is the study of being. Dr. Coakley is suggesting that desire is categorically part of what makes God, God. It's part of God's being. And since Coakley believes that humans are made in the image of God, she's positing that the presence of desire in humans is part of that image. In other words, for Coakley, desire is nothing less than God-given, and *all* desire points back to God in some way or another.

She couldn't possibly be right about that, could she?

Stepping Stones

We are runaways because we desire something.

If Sarah Coakley is right, if desire is part of the beingness of God, and if the presence of desire within humans is part of what it means to be created in the image of God, then the view of humanity preached to me by nearly everyone as I was growing up was suddenly turned on its head. They told me desire *pulls us away from God*, and we must deny desire in order to obey him. They told me God must punish us for our desires but that Jesus steps in and takes the punishment on our behalf.

But what if none of that is true? And what if our desires as runaways are not pulling us away from God but toward her?

It seems we have competing models of desire here.

There's the model I learned as a kid, the one many pastors and politicians preach: The only thing stopping people from lying, cheating, pedophiling, and murdering their way through life is God. In short, desire is bad, and God stands in the way of it.

Then there's the more positive, and ultimately hopeful, model I was learning about at The Seattle School.

A few years ago, I was chatting with pastor and public theologian Nadia Bolz-Weber on my podcast. I asked where she's finding hope when it seems like there's so little good left in Christianity.

"People don't leave the church or Christianity because they stopped believing in the gospel," she said. "People leave the church because they believe in the gospel so much, they can't stomach being part of an institution or a community that says it's about it and so clearly isn't. That's different."[1] She continued:

> The hope I find is in how many people still believe in Jesus even after the institution has fucked us so much. That we are somehow able to separate the institution from the gospel. The fact that people still believe in it and still are reaching for the hem of the garment—the church hasn't fucked it up so much that nobody's doing that—that's incredible to me. I find hope in that. So my hope is: What's the thing within us that causes us to still reach, and what does the hem of the garment represent? That's the core of the hope, not the other stuff.[2]

Bolz-Weber is alluding to a story in the Gospels in which a woman suffering from a disease worked her way through a crowd just to be able to touch the hem of Jesus's clothing and was healed in the process.

Both Sarah Coakley and Nadia Bolz-Weber are playing with an entirely different model of desire. As Bolz-Weber says, desire is "the thing within us that causes us to still reach." No matter how messed up things seem to be.

The model from my childhood characterizes desire as orienting us toward depravity, while the new model I was learning about says desire orients us toward something greater. The first model sets up a split between humanity and divinity, creating opposing categories: Godly desire versus human desire. Renounce one to get the other.

The other model suggests a union: Because God desires, humans desire. They're one and the same. On a fundamental level, human desire will always reflect at least a small sliver of God because desire is in itself godly. Godly in that it is part of God. Desire has an infinite source.

It's taken us half a book to get here, but we're now at the stepping stone many runaways jump to first. The first thing these runaways toss out from their old theological systems is the belief that human beings are fundamentally depraved or evil.

Some of us read the creation myths in Genesis again and stop at the place where God declares all creation, including humans, "good." God never takes that back. She never says, "Oops. Wait, never mind . . . you're all evil," even during what is often referred to as "the Fall" in Genesis 3.

Other people leap to that first stepping stone because they're searching for something other than the theology of shame they were steeped in for years. We ask ourselves: if shame-based theology begins with the assumption that the human heart is evil and degenerate, then shouldn't a non-shaming theology start with the assumption that humans are good?

But here's the difficult thing. If all we do is swap our beliefs about the fundamental badness of humanity for beliefs about the fundamental goodness of humanity, we haven't actually moved very far. Belief in human goodness may help combat the shame-based theology a little bit, but in practice, we are often simply yelling at ourselves, "Just believe you're good already!"

Let's assume we're able to make a further leap onto a second stepping stone and fully believe in our own goodness. We still haven't explored or explained our hurt. We still don't understand why we have to run away, and if we don't know why we're running, we won't find the new environment we need, one where we can thrive.

I think that was part of my reaction when I tried that new church. I was trying to jump to a new stepping stone without understanding the source of my pain. I was searching for a new environment without tending to the parts of me that were still stuck in the old one.

Yarn

I imagine you've had the experience at some point in your life of being an outsider. After all, you're reading this book for a reason. Here's a story about becoming an outsider that is entirely made up and definitely never happened.

Imagine you felt like an outsider one day when you told the members of your competitive crochet club that you were going to learn how to knit. You had hoped they would support you, maybe even allow you to bring some knitting to the club to create fun hybrid pieces. But, quickly, it became clear you'd now forever be known as "the knitter." Each time it came out of one of your friends' mouths, you heard a touch of lighthearted scorn.

"Why don't you just go join the knitting club?" they would ask you, chuckling. Because everyone knew they didn't really knit over there; their club was just an excuse to get together and drink wine.

One day, you took them up on the dare. You got so fed up with the crocheters that you packed up your needles and yarn and marched right over to join the Knit Wits.

They welcomed you with open arms and a glass of wine poured so full it almost spilled. They said your name with delight, not scorn. And you got to share insider intel with them about the affairs of everyone in the Crochet Crowd. Late into the night, you laughed with them until it was hard to believe you ever competitively crocheted. One of the Knit Wits even decided to name their cat after you.

But then it got awkward one day when you ran into a few of the crocheters while picking up wine at Walmart. They eyed the bottles in your cart.

"Your knitting is going well, I see," said one of your old friends with a glint in their eye.

You froze, only managing to respond, "It is!"

Damn crocheters think they're better than everyone else.

Almost anyone who becomes an outsider, separated from their former community, does the same thing: They leave the place where they don't feel welcome and find a new place where they feel accepted. They fully embrace becoming a Knit Wit.

Or a Progressive Christian.

For many people I know, the Progressive Christianity movement removes the shame and discomfort of staying in a place they don't feel they belong, but to me, it looks like they're shifting to the other side of a seesaw. The fulcrum of the seesaw remains the same, and the balance isn't disrupted. To put it in terms of our yarn-centric story: they go from laughing at the knitters to laughing at the crocheters.

In religious terms, we runaways often go from holding in contempt people who believe that humanity is fundamentally good to holding in contempt people who believe that humanity is fundamentally evil.

We have switched sides and, in the process, gained a sense of ourselves as good, but the system is still based on shaming.

Anytime we think in categories of good and bad, drawing lines based on who is inside and outside, shame isn't too far behind. The environment, or the religious system we're in, functions the same way.

Even if the crocheters are objectively assholes.

I See It, I Want It

People tend to swap "sides," so to speak, when looking for a new environment in which to thrive. As we explored in the previous part, it's *hard* for our nervous systems to change environments. It's much more likely when we're taking those first steps as runaways that we'll get caught up in a system that functions the same way as our old system but allows us again to feel like insiders instead of outsiders.

When I was looking for a new church, I was searching for a place that seemed familiar, like the churches I grew up in, but gayer. I kept looking for a long time, but gradually my professors and colleagues at The Seattle School pulled the proverbial rug out from underneath me.

A definitional swap like "humans are good instead of bad" isn't going to do much to help us find a new church community—or a new home outside of church—if we don't first tend to our larger environments. Without a shift in our environment, the same patterns in our thinking will resurface or even intensify. We could get stuck in a system that perpetuates a sense of "goodness" and "badness" in an ever-shifting, ever-fervent frothing of who is inside and outside, who is good today and bad tomorrow.

We've talked about the ways our nervous systems work, the ways we are formed and shaped in relationship to others. But to get a complete picture of what we're up against, we need to understand how human desire works on an individual and a systems level.

In fact, I think understanding desire—what and how you desire—may be the most important part of this whole journey.

Let's pretend for a moment that you and I are doing one of those segments for a TV show where we stick a microphone in a random person's face and ask surprise questions. Think about Billy Eichner's *Billy on the Street* or what late-night TV correspondents do to make fun of opposing political parties.

I'm your cameraperson, and you're asking the questions. Our assignment: figuring out how people chose to buy items they're wearing.

"Excuse me, random person," you say, aggressively blocking someone's stroll down a Manhattan street with your microphone. "Tell me, how did you decide you wanted to buy that Hermés bag you're carrying?"

If you are aggressive enough to get that person to stop, we can imagine what the answer would be. They'd say, "I don't know. I just really liked it!"

Maybe this person had the means to buy it right away. Maybe they saved up for a year to buy it as a birthday present for themselves. Or maybe they found it secondhand, a steal at $10,000.

As you continue to ask strangers on the street how they chose to buy various articles of clothing, a pattern will likely emerge: They saw their coat in a store and had to have it. Or they were at a Casual Corner back in 2003 and fished a sweater from the bottom of a clearance bin, thinking, *Oh, this blue is pretty.*

The pattern emerging is indicative of what many philosophers and cultural anthropologists call a *linear* model of human desire. It's summed up best by Ariana Grande in her 2019 pop hit "*7 Rings*": "I see it, I like it, I want it, I got it."

There's us and the object of our desire, which can be anything. A direct line connects the two: I see something I like; I want it, so I get it.

Generally, we tend to view desire as something that originates within ourselves. We have our own personal styles, aesthetics, things we like and dislike, and we attribute them to our own individuality. We view desire as part of who we are, a defining feature of our larger personalities.

What if we were to press our people on the street a little more?

"Yeah, okay, you liked it. But *why* did you like it? How did you choose between that bag and the one right next to it?"

The question gets a little bit harder to answer.

"I just did!"

"It looks like me!"

Or maybe, "Because blue is my favorite color."

I would've described my choices and my desires in the same way as our interviewees above before I ran across the work of French literary critic turned philosopher René Girard.

Stick with me here. Yes, we're about to dive into some French philosophy, but I promise it's not going to be too painful.

In 1961, Girard published a book called *Mensonge romantique et vérité romanesque*, or, as the 1965 English translation was titled, *Deceit, Desire and the Novel*. In this book, Girard reveals he has stumbled across something fascinating while studying classic literature. He kept noticing that the authors of what are considered some of the greatest literary masterpieces (in the Global North)—people like Miguel de Cervantes, Gustave Flaubert, Marcel Proust, William Shakespeare, Fyodor Dostoyevsky, the list goes on and on—seemed to understand and write from a model of human desire that was vastly different from the model of linear desire that most people take for granted.

Girard called this version of desire *triangular desire* or, later, *mimetic desire*. *Mimetic* in this case essentially means "imitative." His theory introduces a third party into the conceptualization of desire. Girard writes that a person "pursues objects which are determined for him, or at least seem to be determined for him"[1] by a *mediator*.

In a linear model of desire, we know we have two parties: the subject who desires and the object of desire. Girard says no, there's someone else here who is the *mediator* of desire. The bottom line: *desire isn't something that originates entirely within us; we learn what we desire from others.*

In other words, desire is environmentally and communally determined.

An easy way to illustrate this is through advertising. When I was working as a graphic designer, one of the golden rules of marketing and advertising we would repeat was "Get a human in there." Any time we could show a human using a product or in some way improving their life with a product, we would do it. Notice that most TV commercials are filled with smiling people who seem *just so happy!*

Many of us are wise to this tactic by now. We know we're being sold to, and we have enough experience to know most products won't make us that happy. But advertisements tap into something beneath our conscious minds, where our mirror neurons and nervous systems come into the equation.

On a deep level, if we see someone who is happy or impossibly cool or incredibly wealthy, we want that characteristic too. Effective advertising models something far more than a product; it models a narrative, a story in which we see ourselves as the main character.

Girard suggests that desire is not linear but is *reflective*. We see someone who has something, and they model desire to us, and then we want that something too.

Neurons

We can't see our own faces.

If I think about this too hard, which I have, I get stuck in an existential rabbit hole. I've never actually seen my own face. I've only seen a reflection of it or a photograph, but I can't actively see my own face without some kind of assistance.

Our faces reveal a whole lot more about ourselves than we realize, in part because our faces are the only parts of our body where skin is attached directly to muscle. Everywhere else, muscle is attached to tendons and bones. But on our faces, because of this direct skin-to-muscle attachment, even the most minute contractions of those muscles can expose the underlying emotions driving those movements. These muscles of our faces, for the most part, are controlled by our autonomic nervous systems, meaning that most facial expressions are involuntary.

Of course, we can try to force or suppress expressions, but those attempts are usually futile. Unless we've had a lot of Botox, it's difficult to hide how we feel.

With that said, if hiding our emotions from expression was crucial to surviving as children, then we might have difficulty showing *any* emotion on our faces. Remember, our nervous systems adapt to our environments, trying to regulate for safety. If showing emotion is dangerous, our bodies did what they do best and made sure we didn't show what could get us in trouble.

Still, intuitive people are often able to pick up on emotional cues. Perhaps you've done everything you could to hide something that's troubling you. Then someone asks you, "Hey, is everything okay?"

And it's not just our face muscles that reveal our emotional states. It's our entire bodies, and the processes involved are incredibly complex. It doesn't help that we have all these little neurons in the front of our brains, roughly behind our foreheads, called *mirror neurons*. These are neurons that help us read the intentions of others, involuntarily and automatically.

Another way to say this is: mirror neurons help us read the internal worlds of other people, picking up on even the subtlest cues.

Scientists discovered mirror neurons back in the 1980s. A few researchers noticed that if they gave monkeys peanuts and observed what happened in their brains, they could see which neurons fired. Then the researchers ate some peanuts themselves in front of those same monkeys and saw the *exact* neurons that had fired when the monkeys themselves ate the peanuts also fired when the monkeys observed the researchers eating the peanuts.[1]

What did this mean? The monkeys' neurons fired because of their *motor* activation (when they ate a peanut) and also because of *perceptual* activation (when they saw someone else do the same thing). The neurons literally mirrored what was happening in the brains of the humans. These two things together, both motor and perceptual activation, make a mirror neuron a mirror neuron. Researchers have been studying how this works in human brains ever since those first experiments, and they're now discovering mirror neurons may be a reason we experience empathy.

The thing that's important to note is that *our brains learn from experience.* The monkeys observed in this initial study knew what eating a peanut was like because they had experienced eating a peanut. That experience got coded into their neurons. Then when they perceived someone else eating a peanut, those same neurons reacted.

That principle is in play when we're talking about perceiving the emotions of another person. To accurately intuit the emotions of someone else, we first must have experienced and registered those emotions ourselves. The *and registered* part is important. Humans are emotional beings; we are constantly experiencing emotions. But we aren't always aware of them, or we've developed ways to keep them out of conscious perception. We must have worked with any given emotion of our own to be able to work with it in another person. Sometimes this is called *emotional intelligence.* It takes knowing our own internal world to be able to intuit the internal world of someone else.

But there's more to this story, and here's where things get tricky: We can only come to know our own internal world based on the experience we have had with other people. Just like we cannot see our own faces, we cannot intuit our own emotional states without someone helping us categorize them.

This may be a bit confusing to our adult brains because many of us have a functioning grasp of our emotional states, but I want you to think about infant development for a moment. An infant comes into this big, scary world undifferentiated. Some psychologists believe babies initially don't even perceive themselves as separate from their primary caregiver. They are flooded with an onslaught of sensations: cold air, warm air, hunger, voices, touch, smiling people, angry people, exhausted people. All of these things are new and overwhelming.

A good caregiver can intuit what is going on for an infant and slowly, across time, help them categorize experiences. Part of this "intuition" is their *own* mirror neurons firing. Because a caregiver has vastly more emotional experience than their baby at this point, the caregiver's brain is able to perceive the undifferentiated cues the baby is sending out. The caregiver is then able to work with those emotions and describe them back to the baby, helping the baby begin to sort out their own experience. Think of a parent recognizing when their baby is hungry, or angry, or sad and providing care in those moments.

"Oh, baby is angry! Yes, this is so hard!"

Some caregivers are able to do this well, and others are not. For better or for worse, our caregiver's ability has a direct impact on how we then show up in the world for the rest of our lives. The same can be said of that caregiver's caregivers and so on. This is partly how family cultures and systems are created, which in turn create larger systems and cultures. It also is partly how trauma is passed down generationally.

The point is that we are all so interconnected.

Dr. Daniel Siegel describes it this way: "How we come to know 'who' we are is shaped by the communication we've had with others. If that communication has been filled with confusion and unpredictable actions—or filled with hostile intention—then our internal sense of a coherent self will be compromised. In contrast, being around caregivers in life who are attuned to our own internal worlds in a reliable way will provide us with the 'mirror experiences' that enable us to have a coherent and flexible sense of ourselves in the world."[2]

A caregiver who senses the emotional state of their baby and responds in a way that helps the baby make sense of their internal world is how our minds grow. As our minds grow, they become reflective of our caretaker's abilities and responses.

While it is a bit reductive to say it this way, you can argue that every person is a *reflection* of the all the environments they have existed within. This is incredible to me because it means, at a fundamental level, we are not individuals, at least in the way we often think of ourselves as being entirely independent and differentiated from those around us. We are intricately bound to and shaped by the communities that have surrounded us.

"Individualism" is a myth.

We are mirrors.

We are mirrors who need mirrors.

Mind

I use the word *mind* instead of *brain* intentionally throughout this book because I believe our minds are different from our brains. We were born with brains, but minds develop over time.

There's a field of study called interpersonal neurobiology, which sounds impressive, so when I took graduate courses in the subject, I definitely threw the term around pretentiously.

"Oh yes, I believe our minds are different from our brains . . . have you heard of interpersonal neurobiology?"

And here I am doing it again.

The field explores the neurobiology of how humans interact with each other. In short, it's about how our minds develop.

Much of what I've already shared with you comes from this field of study. Everything we've discussed about our windows of tolerance, our nervous systems, and mirror neurons falls under this umbrella.

But what do our nervous systems have to do with our minds? That, my friend, is the fun thing about interpersonal neurobiology.

Scientists in the field define the mind as "an embodied and relational process that regulates the flow of energy and information."[1]

The implications of this are immense, so let's unpack some of them.

Let's start with the word *embodied*. We're already getting far beyond our brains here. Our minds don't just exist in our heads; they include our entire bodies and the systems of intelligence contained within.

Ever since 1637, when the philosopher René Descartes published the words *cogito, ergo sum,* "I think, therefore I am," so-called enlightened thought has peddled the idea that our thoughts, our cognition, are the end-all, be-all of being human. If we can just get control of our thoughts, if we can change our disordered ways of thinking, we will get a handle on our emotions *and* bodies and essentially be limitless. Entire fields of therapy are founded on this idea. But it's not true.

While there is merit in cognitively oriented types of therapy and certainly something to be said about interrogating our thought life so we might develop kinder ways of being, the idea that our thoughts are the control center of our being is simply wrong.

The neuroscientist Antonio Damasio is widely credited with saying, "We are not thinking machines that feel; rather, we are feeling machines that think." For the life of me, I cannot find where he actually said this, but it is a phrase that summarizes his decades of work and writing. Damasio pioneered research showing that human thought and consciousness is organized around feelings and emotions instead of the other way around. But I think Damasio would be the first to admit even that sets up a false binary. The two are inseparable: we feel *and* think. Throughout our whole bodies.

Indeed, there is emerging evidence that our *guts* store certain types of memory in ways similar to the way our brains store memory. These investigations of the neural capacities in regions other than our brains are still in their infancy, but it is safe to say that thought and consciousness are tied to feelings and emotions—to our bodies—far more than traditionally understood.

Embodiment is not just a trendy term; our minds reside in our bodies.

But not just there. The next part of the definition of the mind is (forgive me) mind-blowing: "embodied *and relational*."

We've already looked at mirror neurons and the ways our minds are formed by interactions with others, but this definition opens things up even more. Our minds include relationships. The map of every relationship we've ever been in and the people we are in a room with at any given moment are in our minds. If our minds regulate the flow of energy and information, that is happening in tandem with the operations of every other mind we encounter and every other body we meet.

Again, I want to stress that we are interconnected in ways modern science is only now just beginning to explore.

Our minds work continually to regulate all of the information and energy coming our way and all of the information and energy within us.

Do you see that key word there? *Regulate.*

Our nervous systems certainly fit into that "embodied" category, but more specifically, they fit into the "regulate" part of the definition. As we've already discussed, our nervous systems are the regulatory center of our bodies. They're part of our minds.

If I'm interacting with you, your nervous system is part of my mind, and my nervous system is part of yours.

Trauma therapist Resmaa Menakem describes this in his book *My Grandmother's Hands*, saying, "Although they don't always realize it, people visit my office to be with my settled, regulated nervous system. At first, clients come in with dysregulated nervous systems. Over time, their repeated contact with my nervous system helps their nervous systems settle."

He continues, "What takes place is energetic, chemical, biological—a synching of vibrations and energies. My nervous system does not model the way; over time, it helps other nervous systems access the same infinite source that mine does."[2]

For Menakem, there is a spiritual component at play here too. An infinite source, a source of regulation beyond any one of us. Tapping into that source is an incredibly complex process, a process that requires relationship but that is not limited to relationship.

It's all part of our minds. When I sat in that Seattle church, my pain from all the churches I had sat in before then came rushing back. I couldn't differentiate between *then* and *now* because I hadn't had a regulatory presence in my life yet. My nervous system didn't know the difference between *this church* and all the other faith communities I had been in previously. It couldn't regulate me, so I ran.

Boots

We are *so* dependent on the people around us. You may be tired of me saying this by now, but the environments we are born into are what shape us into who we are. We cannot separate who we have become from those formative contexts.

René Girard describes something about human desire that the field of interpersonal neurobiology seems to be verifying scientifically: There's no such thing as linear desire. Any desire we have within us has been shaped and formed by an infinite web of relationships.

Girard takes this theory of imitative desire and makes it the foundation of a new approach to the way human cultures work. He notes that because desire is triangular, it creates competition for the object of desire and simultaneously sets up a belief in scarcity around the object. And competition and scarcity breed violence. Think of the images we see on TV after Black Friday, people rushing into stores and fighting for deals in small-scale violence that sometimes turns deadly.

Or let's look at a scene from the iconic, but sadly underrated, movie *Confessions of a Shopaholic*. Our protagonist, Rebecca Bloomwood (played by Isla Fisher), has a shopping problem. She's racked up thousands upon thousands of dollars of credit card debt, and in an odd twist of fate, she ends up writing an advice column for a financial magazine. All the while, Rebecca is attempting to avoid the debt collector who is stalking her and kick her shopping habit by attending Shopaholics Anonymous.

Just when it seems she may be getting her shopping habit under control, a stray flyer drifting through the wind lands on Rebecca's coat as she's walking down a New York City street. "Multi-designer sample sale!" it screams.

"At every point, I will ask, 'Do I need this?'" Rebecca vows, getting in line for the sale as people flood out of the warehouse exclaiming, "Gucci! For half off!"

Rebecca's self-control initially seems to hold up. She finds a set of purple cashmere gloves. "Well, these I need," she says to herself, "because it is winter, and I have . . . hands . . . so that's all. I'll buy these and these alone! I walk away. Strong. And frugal."

But then she spots a pair of boots. Not just any boots. Pucci boots. For half off. Red and beautiful. She caresses them while asking, "Do I need these? Do. I. Need. These?"

Her resolve takes over. "No." And just as she's setting them down, another woman rushes up and grabs them, yelling, "Pucci! Pucci boots!"

It's too much for Rebecca. She reaches back for the boots, explaining that she was actually going to get them. She had them first. And if the woman would just hand over the boots, nobody will get hurt. The woman refuses, wrestling the boots out of Rebecca's hands.

Rebecca does what any reasonable person would do: she lunges for the woman's throat.

This, my friends, is a prime example of mimetic desire functioning in all its complexity. Rebecca is torn between two options: the life of an extravagant fashionista and the life she wants as a responsible, debt-free financial writer. When she decides to put the boots back, she's proud of herself and probably thinking about how proud her shopaholic group will be of her.

But the moment Rebecca sees another woman wanting the boots, she's snapped out of it. A newer, more immediate vision takes over: the life of the woman who wants the boots. And now Rebecca knows she *has* to have them. The other woman cannot have them at any cost.

And there's only one pair of boots.

Girard points out that sometimes the scarcity created by competition is real. For example, there really was only one pair of boots at that sample sale. Sometimes it's only perceived, like when a child sees their friend playing with a certain toy and wants it, even though there are many identical toys scattered all round the room.

Girard suggests the primary way we attempt to solve the problem of scarcity is through violence. This can be explicit or implicit violence, and if we look at violence in religious communities, we see both versions. For example, Dr. Parker, whom we met in part 3, outlines in her book *If God Still Breathes, Why Can't I?*, the reality of what she calls "protective strategies," by which she means how white evangelicals keep power. In the United States, this power was once maintained through the explicit violence of enslavement, segregation, and lynching. While lynching still happens at the hands of the State, in many churches, these strategies have become subtler, reinforced by how we understand Scripture. Parker writes that certain doctrines, such as the doctrine of inerrancy, "act as tools of control for the people who normally have the most power over deciding the 'proper' readings of Scripture. These people tend to be a certain group: White male biblical scholars."[1]

Dr. Parker continues, "Anyone who questions or pushes back against these accepted viewpoints becomes disciplined and subsequently ostracized."[2] This form of exclusion and ostracization accomplishes the same thing as the more explicit forms of violence: It keeps certain people in power and others away from that power. By disciplining and excluding anyone who questions certain doctrines, as many Black, Brown, and Indigenous people do, the systems keep functioning as is with the same people dictating "proper" readings of Scripture.

Many of us learn to hide our impulses toward explicit violence over time, manifesting them in much more insidious and cunning ways, including the stories we tell that mask our true intentions from others and justify our actions to ourselves.

Scapegoats

What makes Girard's mimetic theory of desire so alluring to me is not only its simplicity but also its enormous explanatory power. Soon after Girard published his first book, scholars and laypeople alike noticed its significance. It was as if Girard were pulling back the curtain on something new but ancient, obvious but long obscured.

His theory doesn't just explain individual human actions, or why people choose one thing over another. It also explains how human systems are created and maintained. Girard observed that the violence created from what he calls "mimetic rivalry"—the competition of multiple people for a singular object—has a destabilizing effect on the larger culture. The more competition intensifies, the higher the chance of all-out war.

Think about your favorite reality show in which multiple people compete for a single prize. Mine is *RuPaul's Drag Race*.

The competition is pretty similar to every other reality show out there but queerer. The queens arrive at the werk room and at first are relatively friendly to each other. Of course, because the drag community is small, a couple of the queens always have history. Lines are drawn and allies formed, jealousy and envy becoming more and more explicit as the weeks go on. Eventually, all hell breaks loose, usually culminating in a major fight in the werk room. When that happens, RuPaul inevitably pulls out her favorite question as the queens stand together on stage: "Who should go home and why?"

Ru is a shady bitch, and we live for it.

One after another, the queens have to answer the question. Almost always, there's one queen targeted by most of the others, usually the one seen as the source of the drama.

You've seen this before, the way groupthink happens, especially in a competitive environment like at the office, in your family, or in a political campaign. I always find it fascinating to watch how the contestants coalesce around one—sometimes two—other queens.

Girard suggests there's a reason for this pattern. First, there's the imitative quality: It's likely that the person named by the first one to answer the question will be named by the other queens as well. But there's also something else going on, which Girard calls "the scapegoat mechanism."

The concept of scapegoating is a relatively well-understood phenomenon in our culture, describing what happens when a person or group of people is wrongly blamed so others don't have to bear responsibility. The name comes from an ancient traditional practice on the Jewish holy day of Yom Kippur. The high priest would bring out two identical goats (or sheep). One goat symbolically took the place of the Lord and was sacrificed on behalf of the people. To the other, the high priest confessed the community's sins and placed them upon the goat, which then bore that burden for everyone. This latter goat, known as the *scapegoat*, was sent off into the wilderness, sometimes killed, or just allowed to wander. Through the completion of this ritual, the community collectively achieved atonement for their sins.[1]

Girard noticed in his studies of ancient and contemporary literature that the scapegoat mechanism shows up in communities across the world and has an organizing effect. The use of a scapegoat puts a temporary end to competition, transforming violence into peace.

When Ru asks the queens to pick who should go home, usually one queen becomes a metaphorical scapegoat. If the episode's scapegoat doesn't get the sashay, if she ends up staying in the competition—well, things get more than a little awkward.

But if the scapegoated queen does go home, the drama in the werk room momentarily ceases. All the other contestants talk about how much they'll miss that person and wish them the best. These are the same people who just threw the queen under the bus.

This explanation of scapegoating focuses on a big dramatic event. But Girard noticed that scapegoating also happens daily in every society in subtle, barely noticeable ways. We constantly shift blame onto others to relieve ourselves from the burden of responsibility. This happens on an individual level but even more so on a group level. In every human group or community, these dynamics show up, and there's always a victim.

When scapegoating happens on a societal level, the victim isn't just sent away without a crown and prize money. Victims pay a heavy price, including colonization, persecution, segregation, lynching, and genocide. All systems of oppression ultimately hinge on this scapegoat-and-expel pattern.

It's not just that this scapegoat mechanism reveals the underlying violence that is present within human systems; it also reveals the fact that violence *organizes* our societies. We *get* something valuable out of scapegoating if we are not the victims of it. We get order, camaraderie, peace, and meaning. Scapegoating benefits us greatly. In other words, this form of violence has a generative quality.

If we can unite around a shared enemy, or a shared "cause of the problem," or whatever version of "who should go home" we are experiencing, and if we can work together to make sure that person or group of people is eliminated, banished, or otherwise removed from our game, order is created. Community is created. It *feels* really good.

Think of how satisfying it feels when the villain on your favorite reality show *finally* gets eliminated, and you high-five everyone watching with you on the couch or on social media. It's yummy.

While I'm using explicit language to describe these systems, they often function under the surface, in subtle ways that aren't apparent to most participants—especially for those of us who are centered and privileged by society, protected from seeing the victims.

It's easy for us to say, "Well, if you don't want to live on the street, you should get a job." Or, "Enslavement ended 150 years ago. Why are people still upset about it?" Or even, "If you work hard enough, you can achieve anything you want."

All the statements above have something in common. They're all said by people benefiting from the systems they're commenting on.

Because humans create meaning through stories, those who are doing the expelling of a scapegoat always create meaning around the sacrificial event by telling stories that mask what happened. We see such stories play out on the *Drag Race* mainstage if the queen everyone threw under the bus ends up going home and all the other queens talk about how good she was and how much they'll miss her.

Girard says the scapegoat ends up filling dual roles as both the object of intense hatred and, as soon as they are expelled, as an object of awe and adoration. We can see that in many cultures where stories about those expelled become origin myths.

Consider the myth of Thanksgiving celebrated in the United States. It's one of the origin stories of the country: The generous Native Americans helped the English pilgrims survive, they held a great big feast, and everyone lived happily ever after in harmony. This myth masks the reality of how the settlers took advantage of the Indigenous people, exploited them, and massacred them as scapegoats, blaming them for real and imagined suffering.[2] While the earliest colonizers treated Indigenous Americans as their enemy, the Thanksgiving myth, now recounted every November in elementary school classrooms, has become a sanitized narrative of peace and friendship.

Stories told by the victors *always* mask the true violence underneath.

And this is how religions are born.

Us vs. Them

As I learned about Girard and continued to explore interpersonal neurobiology, I finally had language for what I had experienced coming out and what had created the environment I was running away from. It was this scapegoat-and-expel mechanism.

By coming out, I had unknowingly aligned myself with the scapegoats, becoming a scapegoat in my own community. I *had* to be excluded for the system to continue to function. I felt all of this at the time, experienced it, but had no idea how to describe what was happening. I saw myself still as an insider, believing all I had to do was convince everyone else I remained an insider too. But my fate had already been sealed.

Girard helped me understand that the cracking and shattering I was experiencing in my own concrete box wasn't happening by chance. My inclusion, and by extension the inclusion of LGBTQ+ people within my church, would inevitably crack and shatter the entire system because *the system was built on exclusion.*

The system defined itself against certain people: the nonbelievers, the LGBTQs, the feminists, people who believe in abortion rights, etc. If I wanted a faith where people like me could thrive, that faith had to be different from the one I grew up in. There was no room to fold me into my parents' Christianity.

Folding me and people like me in would destroy the very thing creating the group's identity: our exclusion.

Girard helped explain my initial impulses after coming out, my attempts to stay in the fold by assuring the people around me I wasn't like the *other gays*, the ones who believed they could be in relationships. Eventually, I opted for "I'm not like those gays who aren't monogamous." All this positioning propped up the established scapegoat of "those gays" and tacitly assured the people around me, "See, you can still scapegoat *them*. I scapegoat them too."

I should have just worn a badge: *I'm not like them. I'm more like you. Christian, just gay. But not that kind of gay.*

Myths

Shortly after the terrorist attacks on the World Trade Center in 2001, televangelists Jerry Falwell and Pat Robertson took to the airwaves on their show, *The 700 Club*, to explain why the attacks happened. Falwell declared, "I really believe that the pagans, and the abortionists, and the feminists, and the gays and the lesbians who are actively trying to make that an alternative lifestyle, the ACLU, People for the American Way, all of them who have tried to secularize America. I point the finger in their face and say, '*You helped this happen.*'"[1]

Later, in a phone call to CNN, Falwell apologized and explained that he believed the only people to blame for the attacks were the terrorists themselves. But he quickly followed that with "I do believe, as a theologian, based upon many Scriptures and particularly Proverbs 14:23, which says, 'Living by God's principles promotes a nation to greatness; violating those principles brings a nation to shame.'" He named the ACLU again and other groups of people whom he claimed were causing the United States to stray away from its special relationship with God.

"I therefore believe that that created an environment which possibly has caused God to lift the veil of protection which has allowed no one to attack America on our soil since 1812,"[2] he concluded.

How's that for a non-apology?

I've used an anecdote from 2001 because to use one from now would strike a bit too close to home. But the scapegoat mechanism was as apparent back then as it is now. Falwell and Robertson and many others were following the same playbook they usually follow each time a disaster happens. They blame it on the gays and the liberals. Essentially, they argue that if *those people* didn't exist, such bad things wouldn't be happening. It's their fault. If only those people would turn from their evil ways, everything would be better again.

These sentiments aren't much different from the handwritten cards from concerned family members I continued to receive well after my move to Seattle. They explained that I needed to change because I was headed to hell.

Another key point in Girard's theory is related to the use of scapegoats on a grand scale: the birthing of religious systems and setting up the "sacred and the profane."

Because of the unstable nature of mimetic rivalry, the competition and subsequent violence that ensue, humans need a way of reining in that violence so it won't spill over into complete chaos. We avoid chaos by setting up formal systems, including systems of the sacred, which substitutes a *different kind* of violence. Religion is the primary way—but not the only way—we handle this challenge.

All our sacred systems revolve around a type of *intentional sacrifice*. In early human history, human sacrifice prevailed, but later, different types of sacrifice were substituted—first, animal sacrifice, and now it's often symbolic or metaphorical sacrifice.

In order for a sacred system to function, Girard posits that three things must be present: myths, rites, and taboos or prohibitions. Girardian scholar Michael Kirwan explains the function of these three well: "Myths tell the story of the persecution from the perspective of the victor, the lyncher; rites are the controlled repetition of the sacrificial action through which the community gains renewed strength and unanimity, especially where these rites involve sacrifices (victims); taboos and prohibitions are in place so that there will be no repetition of the rivalry which might lead to a new crisis."[3]

Let's briefly look at how Falwell and Robertson's arguments illustrate all three.

1. *The myth of persecution from the perspective of the victor:* Falwell and Robertson stated plainly that 9/11 is the fault of the gays and liberals. God is punishing us because of them.

2. *Controlled repetition of the sacrificial action through which the community gains renewed strength and unanimity:* In the case of 9/11, the violence itself wasn't controlled, but Falwell and Robertson *used* the violence to perpetuate the controlled-sacrificial myth that "God-fearing Americans *like us* were killed because of *you!*" Do you see the ritual here? It's the same ritual that is often used when a person refuses to bake a cake for a gay wedding and claims their religious rights are under attack if they're sued for discrimination. "We are being persecuted because of *you.*" It masks the actual violence that has happened and helps unite people as a persecuted group.

   As a further illustration, let's observe that we repeated the "sacrificial action" on a national level on 9/11 by scapegoating Muslim people. This perpetuated incredible violence against Muslims living in the United States but simultaneously masked the violence by creating a strong sense of national unity through persecution: "We are the victims, not the ones engaging in violence."

3. *Taboos and prohibitions are in place so that there will be no repetition of the rivalry, which might lead to a new crisis:* The prohibitions I'm talking about are likely obvious at this point. Don't be gay, or pagan, or a liberal, or a

feminist, or someone who has had an abortion. These are explicit in Falwell's words: "Living by God's principles promotes a nation to greatness; violating those principles brings a nation to shame." In other words, follow the rules, and a tragedy like this won't happen again.

Do you see how these things all work together to reinforce the goodness of the "in" group and the badness of the "out" group? For this mechanism to be powerful enough to create order from chaos and violence, Girard emphasizes that these three things must be done in the name of the *sacred*. Falwell does just that, appealing to God. "These are not our rules," he's saying. "They are God's, and we are being punished because we have strayed."

While I'm using Falwell and Robertson as an illustrative example of an expansive, prominent system within the United States today, the principles Girard highlights function in *all* systems. The only logic powerful enough to maintain this kind of system is the concept of the *sacred and profane*. There must be something beyond us, beyond just humans, to reinforce the goodness of the in group and on which to blame the violence. The thing beyond humans doesn't have to be religion, the sacred doesn't have to be God, and the profane doesn't have to be sin. It can be as simple as "(sacred) crocheting is objectively better than (profane) knitting."

The stakes are high when you go beyond knitting and crocheting groups. The well-being of any "in" group *depends on a scapegoat and on the creation of the sacred*.

After studying, struggling with, and eventually understanding Girard's revolutionary ideas, I was finally able to put language around my own experience of running away from the in group that told me my desires separated me from God rather than reflecting what was godly in me.

I was also able to see that by calling myself a "runaway," *I was taking part in masking the violence being perpetuated on me* by joining in the myth. For too long, I told myself I was a "runaway," a "lost soul," instead of saying what had actually happened.

I had been kicked out.

Part 5

Slippery Slopes

Wind

Now is when I admit I don't know if I believe God is real. I'm not sure I now believe any of the things I believed so fervently when I was fifteen or twenty or twenty-five. I'm admitting this so you'll understand my perspective as we enter some deep discussions about who and what God is. This is my attempt at putting pieces back together, of saying, "If I believed God is real, here's what I think would be true about her." I want to make sure I'm not posturing or positioning myself as Someone Who Knows Things. Someone who has the Truth all figured out.

It's intimidating to talk about God, especially when we're trying to do that in new ways. A lot of us settle into the zone of "I just don't know anymore." It's honest, and we can stay there comfortably for quite a while.

Recently, I was explaining my work to a new acquaintance, who immediately asked, "So are you still religious then?"

I stumbled and stammered. "Kind of? I'm not sure. Um, I don't really know anymore."

And that was the truth.

This is also the truth: When I'm out walking my dog, listening to the wind in the trees and feeling the warmth of morning sun on my face, I breathe in something that is more than just salty Puget Sound air. Something that is big, elemental, and comforting. And as I exhale, I whisper, "Thank you, Jesus."

Yes, maybe it's a habit from when I was a kid, a reflex. But in the moment, it's a sincere prayer arising from somewhere deep within me. In those moments, I do believe.

But there are other moments when I hear someone say something that reveals their religious faith, something that would have been perfectly normal for me to say a few years ago. Something like: "It seems like evil is trying to hold you back from your calling."

Overhearing this in a coffee shop, I blink, try to make sense of it, and my body jolts as I realize *I don't think that way anymore.*

In such moments, I tell myself I don't believe in God. In fact, I want nothing to do with belief.

And yet there are many other moments when I'm sitting in my office as someone tries to find words to describe horrific experiences of abuse they've suffered. I know then, in the core of my being, that I do still believe in evil.

I harbor so many fragments of a faith that once felt whole, now scattered randomly around me. I can pick one up and look at it, thinking, *This looks pretty! I'm going to hold on to this.* But later I'll trip over one of those fragments and discover it has cut me deeply, painfully. I'll curse and ask, "Why haven't I thrown this away yet?"

My only answer is, "I don't know."

Tom

I think it's Anne Lamott who most often gets credit for saying "You can safely assume you've created God in your own image when it turns out God hates all the same people you do."[1] Although, if you go back and read *Bird by Bird* again, it's her "priest friend Tom" who says this to her.

This part of the book is an exploration of God, rooted in my willingness to say at any point, "I don't know." I'm going to use the word *God* as a default instead of getting more creative with my language. It's a matter of simplicity and familiarity, but if you want to substitute *the Divine* or *Skydaddy* or another term each time you see the word *God*, please feel free.

I will, however, use more inclusive language when it comes to gender as I have in previous parts. I use both *they/them* and *she/her* pronouns for God because I think we need all the reminders we can get that God is not some giant cis white man in the sky—even if your preferred term for them is, indeed, Skydaddy. When I talk about Jesus, I'll continue to use the pronoun *he*.

Priest friend Tom is on to something when he talks about how we mold God in our own image. Lamott's quote still lights up the internet like wildfire. For most of us, posting the "God hates all the same people you do" meme on social media is an attempt to throw a stick in the spokes of *those people*. You know the ones—the narrow-minded, the unkind, the homophobes, the racists—haters of all stripes. I've posted the quote as a giant "fuck you" to a few people from my past who still read my Facebook feed, imagining that priest friend Tom's insight would be the thing leading them to rethink *everything* and then apologize to me.

I'm sure you know that never happens.

But that's our common impulse, isn't it? When we start talking about God, we so often begin from a place that contrasts our kind, understanding version of her with someone else's version that hurts or marginalizes us. If we've been hurt by a specific version of God but somehow still managed to hold on to our faith, it's inevitable we will insist our new God is *different*.

Maybe you've caught yourself saying, full of conviction, "The God I know would *never . . .*" Fill in the blank with a belief you used to hold but have now abandoned. I've said those words more times than I can count.

But as I write this, I must admit that the shift so many people of faith have made from "I believe in a conservative God who hates the homosexuals" to "I believe in a progressive God who hates the people who hate the homosexuals" now, more often than not, leads me extol the virtues of atheism.

Then I hear a whisper. "God doesn't hate anybody!" says Bertha, the name I've given to the fictional sweet, elderly church lady who lives in my head.

"We can play language games all we want, ma'am," I reply. "But whether we say 'hates,' or 'strongly disapproves,' or even 'loves but has a better plan for' really doesn't make a difference. It's semantics."

What I want to explain to Bertha is that when we focus on revising the word *hate*, instead of focusing on what it's describing, it's a lot like when your therapist tells you, "We don't *should on ourselves* in here." Your therapist's goal is to get you to consider all the ways the "shouldn'ts" and "shoulds" in your head *shouldn't* dictate your actions. It doesn't make any sense, and you just end up swapping out different words for the same thing.

"*Shouldn't*—but make it positive!" What is that supposed to mean?

Maybe God truly doesn't hate anybody, but I wouldn't know that by walking into your church, sweet Bertha.

Okay, I wouldn't say that to Bertha's face. Bertha is a gem.

My point in talking about how meaningless language tends to be is that swapping out a conservative God for a more liberal God doesn't end up making much difference. It can take us years to find a version of God that is acceptable as we move away from a God of obedience and toward one who cares about the poor and marginalized. While struggling to change perspectives, most people will ask themselves a follow-up question: "Why do I believe in all of this God stuff anyway?"

It makes sense that many people just stop looking as they face a flood of new and even more challenging questions.

"Do I need God at all?"

"Is God just a made-up story to justify a society's moral code and values?"

"If my image of God can transform so significantly, am I actually finding the 'real' God or just creating them in my own image, as nonbelievers (and, ironically, Anne Lamott's priest friend) accuse me of doing?"

"Wouldn't my life be easier if I just say goodbye to religion and move on unencumbered?"

If I sound like your mom telling you once again that you're on a slippery slope to atheism, it's because I think she's right.

The slippery slope is real, but we're now going to ask all those questions—and more—and find out where the slope ends.

Keys

My guide to asking big questions about God is Fr. James Alison, a Catholic priest and theologian originally from England. Alison has done more than any other thinker I know to flesh out René Girard's understanding of desire and what it means in our shared theological imagination. He's also gay, which, for me, adds a delightful twist to all his work.

Although raised as an evangelical Anglican, Alison was ordained as a priest by the Catholic Church in the 1980s. In 1994, about six years into his service, he had a revelation. "It became clear to me," he writes, "that I could no longer pretend that there was anything wrong with same-sex love."[1]

That realization cost Alison his job. He had to abandon his lifelong dream of being a theologian and a seminary professor in the Catholic Church. He wandered for years, took odd jobs, and wrote several books unpacking the implications of Girard's theory on various concepts of God. He also boldly addressed the problem of the Church's labeling of LGBTQ+ people as "disordered." Eventually, and without ever explaining why, the Vatican ordered him not to teach, preach, or celebrate the sacraments, sending him into a deep depression.

One afternoon in 2017, a couple of months after one of his friends had met with Pope Francis about Alison's plight and his longing to return to his work in the Church, he picked up his phone and heard a soft voice speaking to him in Spanish.

Soy el Papa Francisco. "This is Pope Francis."

After a few minutes of conversation, Alison gradually understood that he was speaking to the real pope, not some prankster.

"I want you to walk with deep interior freedom, following the Spirit of Jesus. And I give you the power of the keys. Do you understand? I give you the power of the keys."[2]

The permanent and unappealable decree that had stripped James Alison of his dreams years earlier was undone with a few words from the pope himself. Alison now had his freedom and universal jurisdiction to preach and hear confessions. His priesthood was reaffirmed.

The Catholic Church had not changed its positions about LGBTQ+ people. What Pope Francis's decision shows us, however, is that *even within the rigid structures of a religious system, something new can emerge through human action.* Alison was set free by the pope's words, in a way practically unheard of before.

"Ignoring canonical regularity, he set me free to exercise my priesthood worldwide . . . I have no canonical superior, no one to whom to be accountable," Alison wrote a few years ago. "At first, I was perplexed by this and the lack of definition it gave me. . . . I began to see that he had chosen not to fit me into an old wineskin but was setting me free to find a place within the new."[3]

This story touches something deep within me. I am not from a Christian tradition that is nearly as hierarchical as Roman Catholicism. Any hint of accountability to something other than a board of elders and a pastor was enough to make people in the churches I grew up in bristle with suspicion. If a pastor said something folks didn't like, they'd just leave. They'd pop into another church down the road and try it on for size.

But I'd be lying if I said there was no hierarchy at all in my church communities. Mine followed lines of gender, age, and race. With cis white men at the top. I followed the lead of my Sunday school teachers, youth group leaders, pastors, and parents; and, in general, men's voices carried more weight than women's. What they approved of and didn't approve of mattered.

Those voices from my past have been hard to silence, their influence hard to shake, especially when I talk about God. I've been happy to leave certain kinds of authorities behind as I've moved forward on my own runaway journey, but part of me still feels torn. I want those authorities from my past to see me, to acknowledge that I'm not abandoning my faith but trying to integrate more into it.

If I'm honest, I want more than acknowledgment; I want their blessing for the different path I'm taking. But I also often think: *Maybe my elders do have it all figured out. Maybe all I need to do is assent.*

If you're a runaway like me, you may long for the praise of a minister you admired or a church elder. I often imagine the flood of relief I'd feel if I got my parents' blessing. I'm rarely even aware I hold a lot of anxiety anymore, in part because I've held on to it for so long—but how wonderful it would be to release it and exhale. What feels like slightly tenuous and potentially dangerous ground now would transform into rich soil where something new could grow. Just with a simple parental blessing, I would be able to say that the people I can't stop caring about believe I'm okay.

Fr. Alison got a blessing and a taste of freedom when Pope Francis called him. That's why I love his story; it's a reminder that those blessings can still come to us, even from the most unexpected people.

I got my own taste of freedom a few years ago sitting in a Chinese restaurant with my conservative childhood pastor after I came out to him. Instead of condemning me, he nodded and said, "I trust you" in a gentle way that made me realize no matter what I decided on issues of theology, he'd be there for me.

But as runaways, we all still yearn for more. Sometimes it seems like we are never fully able to relax after we've wandered. It's difficult for us to talk about God without also talking about the oppressive systems we were part of—and in some ways still are part of—and how they conceptualize God. The more we walk toward a different understanding of God, the more tension we are introducing to those old systems, and that in turn sparks tension within us. If we finally find a new home, it's often at the cost of becoming a stranger in our old home.

To put it simply, we still want and need the words "I trust you" and warm hugs from some of the people we've run from, and it's difficult to make choices that mean those hugs may never come again. If we don't acknowledge this deep part of us that yearns for connection and blessings, it's going to be difficult for us to find a new home that feels like *home*.

I know we should be able to give ourselves our own blessings and that boundaries are important. But deep inside, I think we are tired of crafting those blessings for ourselves. I know I am. We still yearn for people from the world we left behind to help set us free, as my pastor did for me and as Pope Francis did for James Alison.

That doesn't mean we haven't set the right boundaries; it means we are human.

Tethers

Often, it's much easier to remain in the comfortable "I don't know" world than to slide down that slippery slope into the unknown. "I don't know" acts like a rope, a lifeline, to something we do know or, at least, something we used to know. It's a tether between the world we have left and where we are now. And it's much easier to say "I don't know" to people we care about than it is to say "I don't believe in that anymore."

The words "I don't know" carry potential and a hint of reassurance to others that maybe we'll find our way back. "I don't know" also links us to our yearning for blessing. Better to have the *potential* of a blessing from parents, friends, or a pastor again than to take a knife to that rope and be sent careening down the hill.

I hope you can see I'm now talking about two different forms of "I don't know." One is an honest admission of not knowing, which allows us to lean into the unknown with the fullness of our emotional experience: curiosity, grief, anger, everything we hold within us as runaways.

The other "I don't know" is a little less honest, and it's the one I see as a tether between our past and present worlds. It reassures our mothers, fathers, and friends (and maybe ourselves) there might still be hope for us yet. We say it when we *just don't want to get into it*. It's a blind we pull over all our emotions, suspicions, fears, and convictions to maintain a little peace.

As I talk about God in the coming pages, I want to lean into the first kind of "I don't know." To take a journey toward a new understanding, we must first be honest about our own experiences, talking not about what we *wish we believed* about God but what we *actually believe* about God. We must take our own questions seriously.

For me, leaning into this version of "I don't know" means acknowledging I want to believe God is a God of Love, but some of my experiences tell me otherwise. It means letting my doubts come to the surface, with all the anger, sadness, and feelings of betrayal that come with the doubt. I wish I believed that God is working "all things together for good,"[1] but I can't imagine how. Have you felt the same?

I'd like to give you a task now that may be helpful. The goal is to circumvent that second "I don't know," the one we use to dismiss our feelings. Let's be honest about what we actually think and feel instead of settling for what we've been told.

Put this book down for a moment, grab a journal or a piece of paper, and create two columns. In one column, write all the things you wish you believed about God and your own faith. In the other column, write all the things you truly believe at this moment. Write in the form of questions, statements, or even memories—whatever springs to mind.

Take your time.

Avoid easy or glib answers such as "We can't see God's whole plan yet" or "This is where trust comes in."

As you take your questions, statements, and memories seriously, notice what emotion—or absence of emotion—animates your body. Many of us were taught we can't trust our emotions, so much so that they may be difficult to access. But if you're on this runaway journey, my guess is you are experiencing emotions of sadness, anger, and betrayal. Follow the threads of those feelings and write about them.

If journaling isn't your thing, take a moment instead to notice where your thoughts are going as you consider whether there is a disconnect between what you wish you believed about God and what you truly think or feel. Make some mental checkmarks and notes before moving on.

And down the slope we go.

Fragility

I think the slippery slope from "I don't know" to "I don't believe" is real in part because of the big difference between "knowing" and "not knowing." Let me explain: For many of us, the religious communities from which we've come prize "knowing"—or at least a certain type of knowing. Faith, oddly, is often synonymous with certainty.

Here are the things you must believe.

Here's how you're supposed to act.

And here's what you're supposed to say.

The quest to "know"—to find certainty—is different from curiosity (although it would be wrong to say it's not a kind of curiosity). Maybe the quest can be more accurately described as what some psychoanalysts call the "omni-defenses."[1]

You might already be familiar with omni-defenses because many traditions use *omni*-words to describe God: omnipotent, omniscient, omnipresent. Obviously, humans are none of these things, but we easily fall into organizing our emotional experiences as if we were. We believe we know exactly what someone else is thinking when they give us a dirty look, and thus we feel we're omniscient, even though we don't actually know what that person was thinking. Often, kids fantasize their parents' divorce is because of something they did. In other words, they assume they're omnipotent. The kids aren't that powerful, of course, and there are always many factors at play in a breakup. Omnipresence is the fantasy that we must be present in a certain place in order to prevent catastrophe. For example, we feel the only way a work project will get done successfully is if we are there to make sure of it. All these omni-defenses are so common that most of us experience one or more every day, and they can sometimes blur together.

These omni-defenses are all different aspects of a quest to know something with certainty, but why do we call them *defenses?* Because all of them are constructed to guard or defend against a particular kind of pain—the pain we feel when our sense of self is threatened. The technical term for this pain is *persecutory anxiety,*[2] with anxiety being synonymous with pain.

Throughout this chapter, I'm using quotation marks around "knowing" and "not knowing" because both are illusions. We cannot know the things we want to know as if we were omniscient, omnipotent, and omnipresent gods.

But religious certainty, the kind of "knowing" I am describing here, gives us the illusion of being incredibly powerful. Certainty guards against questions and doubt. It helps us organize our emotional experiences and put them into identifiable categories. When we approach the big questions about God and the universe, certainty is especially alluring.

It's much easier on our psyches to "know" something about God than to "not know." "Knowing" gives us a sense of safety, a feeling that we can keep things in order. It helps us be able to say with certainty the difference between "right" and "wrong."

The thing about building an entire belief system or, to be more specific, entire ways of organizing reality on the defensive structures of "knowing" is that this kind of "knowing" is rather fragile. It's a lot like the problems we've discussed about concrete. Our certainty is susceptible to cracking if not maintained under immense pressure.

A little litmus test I can suggest for this type of fragile certainty is the presence of persecutory anxiety. If we've built our reality surrounded by omni-defenses and certainties, when our reality is challenged by someone, we will feel intense persecution. We will feel the person challenging us is personally attacking us, intentionally trying to hurt us, tempt us, and knock us off the righteous path.

Sound familiar?

If *we're* the ones challenging a larger system built on these defensive structures, we're likely to hear people close to us ask, "Why are you doing this to me?"

We become the *persecutors*.

And if we realize that the things we think we "know" we actually *can't* know with certainty, we will start sliding.

Like a slip-n-slide on a steep hill, down, down, down we go on that slippery slope.

Now nothing seems certain, and we will become suspicious of anyone claiming certainty. How can anyone know anything? We realize we no longer can depend on the kind of "knowing" we trusted in the past. That's why I believe the slippery slope from simply asking questions about God to no longer believing is real.

Our downhill slide can be incredibly violent depending on how deeply embedded we were in our system of faith. Unfortunately, the slide won't resemble a fun summer day in our swimsuits but will look more like a painful fracturing and dissolution of our psychic reality.

The suggestion that we might feel disoriented is an understatement. I experienced that disorientation, that fracturing of my own reality firsthand, and then I emerged with a new way of understanding that put the pieces back together.

Contrast

One of my first assignments when I began graduate school was to study a chapter James Alison wrote about atonement theory. I didn't understand a word of it. While my entire homeschool and Christian college education could be described as theological indoctrination, that hadn't prepared me to read the kind of theology birthed in the academy.

Despite my initial confusion, James Alison's work caught me at the right moment to turn my faith on its head and eventually reverse my slide toward "I don't believe." This didn't happen quickly. The revelations took years and years of studying and interrogating Alison and other scholars, but in that first encounter, I made a mental note: "Someday, when I'm a bit more practiced at this kind of reading, I want to return to this."

With a couple of master's degrees under my belt, I finally returned to Alison, and as I made my way through his body of work, I noticed he kept returning to a central, paradoxical concept: atheism offers a more adequate picture of God than theism.[1]

To be clear, Alison is not an atheist. But he believes that if God is God, then God is much more like "nothing at all" than "one of the gods."

If you're not confused by that statement—good for you. Because I still get confused every time I enter these deep, murky waters.

Alison gets to his belief about the power of atheism in a couple of different ways. The first is by exploring the meaning of the word *monotheism*, the belief that there is one God and one God only. Jewish people were the first to adhere to a monotheistic faith, and later Christians and Muslims adopted the concept as their own.

In the Christian monotheism I grew up with, God is the *only* God, in contrast with all the other gods of the ancient Near East, Africa, Asia, and beyond. Alison explains this understanding of the one God as "merely a uniquely big, powerful, and somewhat lonely member of the series 'gods,' all of whose other members have been declared inexistent."[2] And that was pretty much how I understood it.

I was taught to believe that all the other gods in the Old Testament; all the gods in ancient Greek, Roman, Norse, Native American, and other mythologies; all the other gods in any other religion on any continent aren't real. In the most generous interpretation, they don't exist; at worst, they are all demons taking our attention away from the voice of the one God.

Because Alison understands how humans work from a Girardian perspective, he believes that we derive meaning through definitions created by comparison. For example, the statement, "It tastes like chicken" is a comparison that creates meaning. We compare something we don't know (mystery meat) to something we do know (chicken) as a point of reference.

Truly powerful meaning—the kind of meaning that can move people toward action like almost nothing else—is created by defining through comparisons over and against something else. This is *oppositional meaning*. For example, "I will never be like my father." I have defined the meaning of my life as "not my father" (and by extension, I am better). Powerful meaning is created through comparisons like this, which are often followed by feelings of self-righteousness.

As I read about this form of meaning creation, I couldn't help but think about my parents and all the ways I had been trying to get them to see me as valid. A couple of years before, I had sent my dad a book that unpacked the validity of same-sex relationships from a scriptural perspective. We video called mere days after he had received it. I asked him what he thought of it.

"I'm not going to read it," he replied. "I already know what I believe. I have the Bible. I don't need another book."

I couldn't understand that response. Here I was, his son, begging him to open his mind and consider he might be wrong about something. He was flat out refusing.

If I ever have kids, I vowed, *I will not do this to them. I will have an open mind. I won't shut them down.* This thought started to fuel me, propelling me deeper into studying theology. I was creating a form of meaning that I thought was differentiating me.

Inconveniently, Alison and Girard argue that any meaning created through an over-and-against comparison like "I'm not my father" is ultimately futile because it's a form of projection. Alison writes, "What this usually means is, 'I pick up in the other what I do not see that I dislike about myself and use it to define who the other is, and who I claim that I am not.' This leads to self-definition over and against the other, and works equally in the case of individuals, and of groups of whatever size."[3]

Alison is describing classic projection, what happens when we locate certain parts of ourselves that we don't like in other people and then react against them. If we see something we don't like about ourselves in another person (e.g., when I saw my dad's obstinance), we react. Often saying something like "Thank God *I'm* not like that."

Alison fleshes this out one step further, explaining that any time we create meaning through an over-and-against mechanism, we reveal how *similar* the things we are comparing rather than how *different* they are. For example, when I vowed never to be like my father, the truth was I get a lot of my own determination from my dad. This doesn't negate the fact that my dad's reaction to reading that book was incredibly painful and misguided. But if we widen our lenses a little bit, Alison was helping me see that my dad's self-righteousness is coming from a similar place as my own fears. I'm searching for my own theological assurances to cling to. My dad had found his. This in itself isn't a bad thing. But I was creating so much meaning out of it, calling myself "open-minded" and my dad "obstinate" when we were both stuck on opposite ends of the court, unwilling to move.

Returning to God, Alison argues when we attempt to understand the idea of "one God" through an over-and-against comparison to "other gods," our one God ends up being much more like the other gods than different.

In other words, we derive our understanding from *what we already understand and know* so that although we declare something is different, unique, special, and one of a kind, it is not.

Now let's return to my runaway journey as an example that may inform yours.

I was taught that all gods other than the Christian God were murderous, angry, bloodthirsty, and evil—not worthy of worship or adoration. My God was none of those things. My God was a God of love and mercy, better than everyone else's. Because they don't exist anyway.

And yet this "God of Love" also had an overpowering need for justice, obedience, and, ultimately, for punishment.

The faith I grew up with had many ways of explaining how love necessitates punishment, but let's look at this through Alison's lens. If the over-and-against mechanism is true, my God is similar to all the other murderous, angry, bloodthirsty, and evil "other gods," not different.

Strip away all the fancy arguments about the inherent goodness of God and look at the stories of punishment and destruction we learned in Sunday school. I was taught they literally happened. That time God sent a flood and killed the majority of the earth's population, yup, that happened. Or those times God sent plagues upon an entire people group or killed a couple of people because they lied. Also literal truth. In my experience of Christianity, we did have a murderous, bloodthirsty God, but that murderousness was disguised in different language. Language about grace, love, mercy, and salvation. "At least God spared the right people."

At the end of the day, though, you'd better watch out. You don't want to get on God's bad side.

Nothing

As a runaway, I found the swap of a conservative God for a progressive or liberal God unsatisfying. At the core of it, I felt this was just recreating the same faith system but switching up who was in and who was out.

Look at the constant arguments about religion on social media. It seems every person, no matter which side they're on, uses the same appeal: "Just wait until you meet God; then you'll see I'm right!"

James Alison says there's another way of understanding "one God" that is different from an over-and-against comparison to the "other gods." Instead of contrasting our "one God" with "other gods," we can instead contrast God with nothing. He writes, "There is another use of the word 'one,' which is not properly speaking a numerical use at all. This is where 'one God' is opposed to 'nothing.' In other words, where 'one' is more like the exclamation 'is!' than it is like a number. The exclamation 'is!' is opposed to 'nothing there!'"[1]

Instead of comparing God to the "other gods" or understanding God from the standpoint of what we believe a "God" should be, Alison is saying we can understand God as over and against nothing at all. And if you remember our discussion in the previous section, this means God is more similar to "nothing at all" than different.

If we follow Alison's logic, defining our progressive/liberal God over and against their conservative God means our progressive God is much more similar to their conservative God than different. For example, we both see our Gods ultimately proving to the "other side" they were wrong all along. This sense of absolute confidence that our side is righteous and Truthful and good can be hard to maintain over time in a world of pain and suffering, unless you look away from a lot of the pain and suffering. This may be why so many people who find a progressive God end up later just leaving the church and their faith altogether.

Let's return to Girard for a moment. He tells us that our impulse to create the sacred originates in a need to shore up our own identities. It's our cosmic projection of who is in and who is out, who blesses those who are in and curses those who are out.

Sooner or later, we realize it's the same system, whether we pray to the most conservative evangelical God or the most progressive.

I am not saying our values are the same or that there aren't important particularities at stake. There are vital distinctions here, and this is not an attempt to whitewash political lines and say, "We're all the same! Progressives, liberals, conservatives— no difference here!" We aren't the same in how we see the world or what we prioritize in an ideal society. However, for the most part, the ways our economic, political, and social systems *function* behind our differences are similar. Humans are humans.

Alison reasons that God must be so far outside our human system of understanding that we have no accessible point of reference. And that's why our human understanding of "nothing" is far more revealing of God than our understanding of "something."

But again, humans are humans. So how do we even begin to understand a God that's like "nothing"?

Weakness

A few weeks before the 2016 election, I posted on Facebook the words from a song by a band I was really into at the time, The Brilliance. The line was *"Jesus, come in your weakness. Bring hope to all the world."*

At that point, I was often posting on Facebook to get a rise out of people; it was one of my favorite pastimes. But this wasn't one of those times. The words of that song brought my anxious soul a lot of hope as I faced the uncertainty of the impending election. It felt like a pretty normal thing to say.

Until the comments started rolling in.

"What do you mean by Jesus's weakness?"

"In my weakness HE is strong."

"I couldn't worship a weak God."

Those comments made me realize I was coming to the table with a different assumption about Jesus than many of my Facebook friends and acquaintances. And I hadn't even recognized I had changed my thinking.

I had been taught to think about Jesus as *strong*, a *victor* who smashed our enemies of sin and death and who would return soon to *destroy* everyone who doesn't believe in him, ushering in an eternity of peace. In short, the Jesus I learned about in Sunday school put the bad guys on notice; they were finally going to get what they deserved.

But by 2016, I had made a shift, although not necessarily a conscious shift. I no longer imagined Jesus as a tough guy or a victor over the bad guys.

The shift in my thinking started when I met James Alison at a conference, and he helped me start to embrace the "nothingness" of God. Alison said he didn't believe most of the things I had understood as the Truth about God my whole life. He didn't believe that God required sacrifice or that Jesus came to earth to pay a penalty for our human sins.

I'm sure I looked like a stunned deer in headlights. This was one of my heroes, a leading Christian theologian, and he didn't believe Jesus died to pay for our sins?

"Jesus didn't show up to satisfy God's righteous bloodlust," he said. "Instead, humans were the ones who required that sacrifice. *We* were the vengeful ones who needed the spilling of blood. Not God."

It took a while for this new way of understanding Jesus to sink in. Alison was saying that Jesus walked willingly into a human world defined—as it still is today—by violence and dependent on scapegoats. And sure enough, Jesus became the scapegoat. He was murdered not because God wanted or needed his sacrificial death but because as humans, when the stakes are high, we determine who is in and who is out through violence and death.

But Jesus interrupted the system, threw a spanner in the works. He walked into human society, was brutally murdered, and then he broke the system because what was supposed to happen didn't.

The scapegoat didn't stay dead. And the victors, in this case, didn't get to write the only version of the story.

The scapegoat came back to life and told a different story, a truer story, a story about life and love. And through his story, Jesus revealed our ideas about God had been wrong all along.

God and Jesus are *nothing* like the violent and vengeful world we live in.

Punishment

As I said, it took me a while to wrap my head around Alison's new ways of thinking about Jesus. My idea of Jesus was more aligned with what the Old Testament prophet Isaiah says to the oppressed Israelites in Isaiah chapter 49.

The Israelites were in captivity under the Babylonian empire. They had lost everything, including their land, which was their identity. They thought the Lord had forgotten about them, abandoned them.

Through the prophet Isaiah, God assured the people they hadn't been forgotten. And then God made a promise: "For thus says the Lord, 'Even the captives of the mighty shall be taken, and the prey of the tyrant be rescued, for I will contend with those who contend with you, and I will save your children.'"[1]

Here comes the good part. God then says, "I will make your oppressors eat their own flesh, and they shall be drunk with their own blood as with wine. Then all flesh shall know that I am the Lord your Savior, and your Redeemer, the Mighty One of Jacob."[2]

Gross, right?

Unlike the way many Jewish people read this text, I always believed these verses in Isaiah were a prophecy about Jesus. That's what my church community got excited about. A Messiah was coming who would show the rest of the world who's the boss, who would *punish* all the nonbelievers.

Even now, when I get a Facebook message or email that starts with "I didn't want to send this, but I just really feel like the Holy Spirit is telling me to write you and let you know how wicked your life is," I would love to reply with something like "Go eat your own flesh, asshole."

As a kid and teenager, I always loved Burn-It-to-the-Ground Jesus. Who am I kidding? That version of Jesus still appeals to me. I want the Jesus who will punish every single person who has used their Christianity to justify homophobia, transphobia, sexism, racism, ableism, and oppression.

I want the Jesus who is cosmic arbiter of right and wrong, the one my dad believes in but who will ultimately say to me, the righteous Matthias, "Well done, my child. You're right, and your dad has really gone off the rails."

Then he'll turn around and say to the people I think are Really Bad, "Get out of my sight, fools! I never knew you!"

Yes, I get a sense of smug satisfaction thinking about that. It feels good to imagine getting to the afterlife and watching Jesus put the assholes in their places. I relish the image of their faces as they realize how wrong they got it, how futile their efforts to regulate other people and their bodies really were. I want Jesus to take each Bible verse someone used to demean my existence and turn it around on them in a dramatic way that makes them cry.

I tell myself I'm not heartless. I don't want Jesus to *eternally* condemn most of those folks—in part because I fear a new slippery slope in which I cheer the damnation of way too many people. But, in the same breath, there *are* a few other people I can think of that I would like to see eternally condemned. Most of them are the people who have been in my prayers since 2016: "Dear Lord, would it be too hard to send just a little heart attack?"

That's the kind of thing God does, right? And Jesus was just an extension of that energy. He didn't manage to punish the right people on his first go around, so my church family and I figured that just means he'll do it when he comes back.

There's a consistency across Western cultures in that assessment. While the particularities may be different, the function of a "God" in our way of thinking is to reward or punish on a grand level, to save or condemn.

But, as James Alison convinced me, Jesus didn't follow directions. That's not the Jesus we got.

Flesh

The disciples were human, so they were probably hoping for a vengeful, take-no-prisoners Jesus too. They certainly didn't understand God as more "nothing" than "something."

Jesus was performing all those miracles, and rumors were going around that maybe he actually *was* the Messiah they were waiting for—the one who would overthrow the Roman empire, making Roman soldiers eat their own flesh and drink their own blood like a real God.

Crowds were following him around, making him a bit of a celebrity. In Scriptures, it seems the disciples were starting to get some hints that maybe *this was it!* Maybe it was almost time for a big battle, a war between Good and Evil.

One night, everything changed for the disciples, and it's a scene that almost mimics reality TV today, minus the drag makeup:

The disciples and Jesus were all lying around a big table, feasting and preparing for Passover. (People lounged at low tables to eat back then.) As they were eating, Jesus casually decided to throw some drama into the mix, announcing, "Truly, I say to you, one of you will betray me."[1]

The disciples were understandably unnerved. They looked around at each other suspiciously, I imagine, wondering who it was going to be. Just then, Jesus and Judas reached into a dish, and both grabbed some food at the same time.

Jesus made eye contact with Judas, accusing, "He who has dipped his hand in the dish with me will betray me."

Judas played innocent, despite having made a deal with some priests earlier that day to deliver Jesus to them. But Jesus called his bluff, and something really interesting happened. Instead of forcing Judas out of the fold, thwarting his plans, Jesus grabbed some bread and broke it. He handed it out to all his disciples, saying, "This is my body. Take. Eat."

This is my body.

This is my flesh.

I hear the words of Isaiah echoing loudly in the room: "I will make your oppressors eat their own flesh."

This is my body.

This is my flesh.

Take. Eat.

You are the body of Christ.

Jesus then grabbed some wine and passed it around the table. "Drink of it," he insisted. I always imagine he looked at Judas again as he said, "All of you."

"For this is my blood of the covenant, which is poured out for many for the forgiveness of sins."

This is my blood.

Drink.

I hear the echoes again. "And they shall be drunk on their own blood."

As the events of the evening unfolded, the disciples found themselves in a garden with Jesus, surrounded by an angry crowd armed with swords and clubs, led by none other than Judas.

Imagine this scene: Darkness, chaos, fear, betrayal, hurt, and exhaustion. With an army of people closing in.

If I were a disciple, I would think this was it. Surely, this was the beginning of the war to end all wars. Cue the lightning and thunder.

One of the disciples pulled out his sword, ready to begin fighting, and cut off the ear of the high priest. The moment everyone was waiting for. The revolution of the people! Now Jesus would whip the crowd into shape and lead them into battle against the empire!

But no. Instead of grabbing a sword, Jesus took the fallen ear, held it up to the man's head, and healed him.

Jesus then looked around at his disciples and said, "Put your sword back into its place. For all who take the sword will perish by the sword."

From this moment, the disciples' world descended into a living nightmare of excruciating pain and loss. Their leader and a man they loved, the supposed Messiah, the one who was supposed to be an all-powerful agent of God, who could save them from oppression, fell victim to the oppressors. Tortured and murdered.

Jesus, the man who had so much promise and showed so much power through his miracles, was shown to be unbelievably weak. He wouldn't fight. He wouldn't talk. His final days became so embarrassing that some of his disciples denied ever even being associated with him.

I imagine the devastation of those disciples in that moment as they saw their own weaknesses and fears in Jesus's actions that night. It turns out the Messiah was only a human. Nothing more. A human who could die just like them. A human who wouldn't even stand up for himself.

Fools

James Alison taught me how to understand the story of Jesus's death and resurrection in a way that gave me hope and a little faith for the first time in a long time—the kind of hope and faith I'd been seeking for years as a runaway. He turned the story I'd been taught all my life upside down and revealed its full meaning.

Before we talk about the resurrection, I'd like you to imagine one more scene:

You're one of the disciples waking up the morning after Jesus's murder. You rub the blurriness out of your eyes and face the sinking realization that everything that happened the day before wasn't a dream. The man in whom you had placed all your hope for the future is dead. Gone.

I think I would have felt so ashamed, so foolish. I certainly would have cried for the loss of my hero and friend, but I also would have cried and raged for myself. I would have sat in the harsh morning light and wondered what I had been doing all that time, following Jesus, wasting so many good years of my life.

In the end, the oppressors had won. Not only that, but Jesus had *let* them win. He didn't even try to stand up to them, didn't try to fight back.

Many people have explained away this part of the story, reminding me that Jesus had shared with the disciples that he would soon die and be resurrected. As if being told by someone, "I am going to die and come back" would lessen the impact of seeing that person brutally murdered.

That kind of explanation has always felt like spiritual bypassing to me. I don't buy the claim that the disciples somehow didn't experience the horror, betrayal, and grief of watching the man they thought was going to lead a revolution be murdered without attempting to fight back. I don't believe that somehow *this* was the moment they believed Jesus's death was just temporary.

Sure, maybe some of them could remember Jesus's words about "resurrection from the dead," or maybe some of them could remember the time Jesus brought his friend Lazarus back to life. But I doubt they were sitting on the edges of their seats waiting for him to suddenly reappear, especially after watching the bloody crucifixion.

They had already been made fools once that weekend, and they had to be afraid they'd be the next targets—hunted down and murdered for following the dead prophet.

Some traditions and theologians call this period of devastation between Jesus's death and resurrection Holy Saturday. But I'd never been sure why a day of fear when all hope was lost should be labeled "holy" until I looked at it from Fr. Alison's point of view.

Remember that Alison says *we* are the angry divinity, the ones who must have a scapegoat. "*We* are the ones inclined to dwell in wrath and think we need vengeance in order to survive," he explains. In Jesus's death and resurrection, "God was occupying the space of *our* victim so as to show us that we need never do this again."[1]

Like many of you, I grew up believing in a God that required vengeance and that humans were satisfying God's need through our participation in Jesus's death and resurrection. But what Jesus accomplished on earth, according to Alison, was to reveal who God truly was: "God was entirely without vengeance, entirely without substitutionary tricks; and that he was giving himself entirely without ambivalence and ambiguity for *us*, towards *us*, in order to set *us* 'free from our sins'—'our sins' being our way of being bound up with each other in death, vengeance, violence and what is commonly called 'wrath.'"[2]

Having begun this part saying I'm not sure I believe in God, I now want to tell you why the kernel of belief I still hold on to hinges on the literal resurrection of Jesus. If I believe in God, which I'm not sure I do, a literal resurrection of Jesus is incredibly important to that belief for me.

The skeptic and intellectual in me is sometimes embarrassed by my attachment to the "He is risen" story. And I certainly don't think you need to believe in a literal resurrection to follow Jesus's teachings. There's a broad array of interpretive traditions around the resurrection you can choose from, despite what many Christians try to tell you.

For me, though, Alison's argument that the resurrection frees us from the human bondage of death, vengeance, and violence is powerful. And for me, believing in the resurrection moves Jesus's teachings out of the metaphorical, spiritual realm and into the physical world, where I live—the fleshy, sensory world in which I hear leaves crunch under my feet, feel wind against my face, taste salty air, and breathe out, "Thank you, Jesus."

My faith is no longer an act of abstract theological assent, an idea. It is about action. Something out of the ordinary has happened, and that action has had an impact in an actual place and time, on an actual human body.

If Jesus died and came back to life, something so real happened that I don't have to *believe*; the act has been *done whether I believe or not*.

Instead of a story about God visiting earth in the form of a human named Jesus, who then leads a revolution against God's enemies to establish some sort of godly kingdom on earth, God is the one who dies. There is no revolution. At least not in the way we think about revolution.

Instead of a story in which God scapegoats the entire human race in order to maintain their own identity, making their "goodness" dependent on being over and against the "badness" of humans, instead of requiring humanity to pay for some mysterious offense with violence, God themself becomes *our scapegoat.*

And then they undo the entire system by not staying the scapegoat. The scapegoat comes back to tell the story from a different perspective: the perspective of the victim of the system. And that story reveals the system for what it is: a system bound inextricably to violence and one that is entirely human.

When Jesus resurrects, a victim returning from his horrific death, he is the Divine holding up a mirror to us and saying, "Look! Look at who you are. But you don't have to be this way."

Collapse

Many of my friends and colleagues question the relevance of faith in their daily lives, especially now, as we seem to be in the midst of a great societal collapse. The wealthy are more willing and able than ever to seize and keep their power, no matter the cost to the poor and suffering.

As I've been writing this book, I've also been questioning the relevance of my own faith. I sit on my couch with my laptop and see awful news story after awful news story. I fear what is going to happen to the earth, what is going to happen to my friends, and what is going to happen to me, and I feel powerless. The politics of hate seems to be the new reality, the new "normal," so I ask myself, "Why even bother with this faith stuff? What good is it?"

And yet I've continued to get up every morning to think and write about my faith and have arrived at a new understanding of Jesus and a new understanding of the way of the victim. That new understanding now feels robust enough to address the question that is the subtext of this whole part of the book: *Why bother with God?*

The new story I want to tell, inspired by James Alison's reading of the resurrection, is about hope for what is happening in our world today.

Remember the metaphor of the concrete boxes from part 2? I believe the resurrected Jesus looks at those boxes we humans are trapped inside, tells us they are held together only by the pressure of violence, and shatters them.

Through his death and resurrection, Jesus shows us that all social, political, and religious systems and hierarchies are fundamentally violent. But he doesn't leave us bereft; he introduces another way of being—the way of the victim. The way of the scapegoat.

By his own example, Jesus reveals that those of us on the periphery, who live on the edges of human economic, political, social, and religious systems of oppression and become scapegoats and victims, are the most qualified to tell the truth about the systems in which we are trapped.

And we who are runaways are even freer than most scapegoats and victims because we no longer benefit from those intact religious hierarchies and structures. From a distance, we see them clearly and without blinders, revealing all their cracks and holes.

Jesus invites us to listen to the victims of psychological and physical violence and, more important, to participate *alongside them* in revealing the truth about the violence. After listening and joining together in sharing the truth, we're on a slippery slope toward inevitably shattering the concrete boxes, the structures that trap, confine, and silence us. The shattering will be violent, and the boxes will collapse.

They must collapse even if we don't know what will take their place.

Why do I have more hope now than ever, given all this necessary violence and shattering and collapse? Because I now think I know what to look for as evidence that something new is appearing in the midst of despair and chaos, like a small plant growing and cracking the concrete around it.

For me, that evidence is that victims and scapegoats are being listened to more now than ever before in all human history.

Part 6

Pain

Heartbreak

A year or so into my time at The Seattle School, I was invited to pop across the US/Canada border to speak at a small conference of LGBTQ+ people of faith. The retreat location was romantic, in the full sense of the word, nestled in the stunning, pine-covered mountains of British Columbia. I was primed and ready. As I wandered around the retreat center, someone kept catching my eye. We'll call them Aspen.

Like a lot of people, when I see someone hot, I'm immediately intimidated. My flirting strategy is summed up in three words: *hide and avoid*. I sneak glances at the person from across the room and hope they notice me. If they do notice, my face always turns bright red, and I look away immediately. With no disrespect, I would say I have a middle-school-girl approach to flirting, and it rarely works out well. You're not surprised?

But on that Canadian retreat, something aligned in a new way. When I gave my talk on the last night of the conference, Aspen sat in the audience directly in my line of sight. Making eye contact was unavoidable, and as a result, I kept getting distracted, losing track of what I was saying. I could feel my face turning deep red several times as I mustered all my powers to *focus* and get through the talk.

I stepped off the stage knowing I was smitten. Resistance was futile.

I set my first goal: try speaking to them that evening. The opportunity presented itself almost immediately. Aspen came up to me at the meet-and-greet after my talk and asked if I was going to join the rest of the twentysomethings at the local bar that night. My face again flushed warm and red. I said *yes*.

We had a lovely evening together, and as I went to back to my little cabin in the pine woods that night, I kept wishing I had made a move to kiss them. I peeked my head out of my cabin door more than once, looking around the camp in the moonlight, hoping Aspen would appear with the same desire.

They didn't.

I drove away from the retreat the next morning with a major crush, still wishing I had expressed my feelings, knowing I had met someone special. The next night, I worked up the courage to slide into Aspen's DMs.

"I wish I had kissed you the other night."

"Me too."

I was on a bus back across the border the following weekend for a proper date. Over the next couple of months, we each made several trips back and forth. I was swept up in a fantasy, the way only a first relationship can completely capture your imagination. Within a month, I was researching how hard it would be to move to Canada after I got my degree. This was it, I thought. Aspen was the one.

Reminder: I was preparing to emigrate roughly six weeks into my first romantic relationship. That didn't matter to me; it felt so *real*.

As I was packing for a visit the week after Christmas, Aspen called and broke up with me. I was blindsided—even though, in retrospect, all the signs had been there the last time I'd seen them. I couldn't wrap my mind around it; this wasn't the way things were supposed to be.

To say I was hurt doesn't really cover it. My heart had split open, and the only thing I could feel was searing pain. Pain that was so intense, I couldn't understand how it could all come from a single heartbreak—and from someone I'd known only a few months.

The pain lasted more than a year. I spent session after session processing the breakup with Solomon, my therapist, trying to figure out what had happened, where we had gone wrong. Trying to figure out why it hurt so much.

I blamed Aspen for everything while simultaneously trying to analyze what I had done wrong. Some of you can probably relate. I kept looking for one uniting piece of the puzzle, the one thing I could have done differently that would have convinced Aspen I was worthy.

I thought Aspen had betrayed me, but neither of us knew what we were doing. It was the first relationship for both of us.

Eventually, Solomon gently started putting together the pieces of my story in a different way—not the way I thought things had happened at all. He constructed a new picture of my heart, a heart that wasn't fresh and untouched as I described it but had known many heartbreaks in the past. Those past heartbreaks didn't happen with romantic partners but instead involved other people in my life who were supposed to care for me. As it turned out, my heart, shattered so many times before, was being held together by the duct tape of sheer willpower and positivity. The perceived betrayal by Aspen had ripped off the tape.

Every betrayal I had ever experienced, and all the grief I had never processed, was funneled through that breakup, which allowed me to feel every ounce of pain inside me, pain that had never before found release.

What initially felt like a confusing, disproportionate response slowly began to make more sense as I understood what I was actually grieving. Sure, I was still sad and mad about Aspen, but the breakup wasn't at the core of my pain.

When all the pieces slid together, I saw, to my surprise, that my parents were at the core, along with the friends who had cheered for my loneliness. The people who suddenly turned on me when I came out were there too. The breakup with Aspen was the final little push, the proverbial straw on the camel's back, that brought me face to face with an overwhelming pain I had done everything I could to hold at bay for years.

I couldn't avoid it any longer.

Fragments

You can't go with others any further than you've gone yourself.

I encountered the phrase above often at The Seattle School but only understood it fully after my breakup, when Solomon helped me understand that I hadn't gone very far myself at all. I had never dealt with much of the pain I had been through. And in the wake of that relationship with Aspen, I learned to connect lessons from my academic studies about trauma with situations in my own life.

One of my professors and mentors, Cathy Loerzel, describes three unmistakable hallmarks of someone with trauma: *fragmentation, isolation, and dissociation*.[1] Many of the symptoms of post-traumatic stress disorder (PTSD) fall within these three categories.

Because I had studied under Cathy, I knew that *fragmentation* is what happens when a traumatic event isn't met with care and integration. We talked a little bit about this phenomenon in the conversation about windows of tolerance in part 3. When we've experienced something that takes us outside our window, it can become traumatic if we don't have another person who can help us understand and integrate our experience. Otherwise, the experience will quite literally *fragment inside us*. If the event is extreme, we'll lose our memory of it or only be able to remember parts of it. Other parts, including the feelings our bodies experienced, will be stored and coded in places where we have no language. Cathy describes it this way: "We are very good at surviving, and while fragmentation is a key survival strategy our brain uses intuitively, it destroys understanding the memory and fails to dislodge the trauma from our body. Fragmentation creates disparate memories that require us to choose between our body's memory or our mind's memory."[2]

In other words, we create stories as an attempt to understand what happened, but the trauma doesn't get resolved; it gets lodged within us.

Isolation often follows fragmentation because when we've experienced a traumatic event, we almost always blame ourselves first and experience shame. We tell ourselves, "I shouldn't have been walking down that street after dark." Or, as I was doing during my breakup, we replay every minute interaction with the ones we love to find the most likely reasons they broke up with us. We scold ourselves: "I shouldn't have asked them to make our relationship official so early; that scared them away."

When shame leads to isolation, we pick apart our actions and vow we'll never do this or that thing again. We imagine we're learning from our experiences, twisting the shame into something positive, but in fact we are closing ourselves off from connection with others. I knew all this from my studies but didn't—or couldn't—apply it to myself.

Fragmentation and isolation inevitably lead to *dissociation* because we physically cannot handle the immensity of what happened to us. We must numb the pain somehow, and in the absence of care from another person who can help us integrate, we develop ways of soothing ourselves. Cathy tells students this can be as simple as watching TV to take our minds off things or as complex as firmly denying anything bad happened to us. We might use willpower to try to forget and "move on." All these strategies fall into the category of dissociation.

Before working through my own pain with Solomon, I could have told you these truths, but they were all theoretical. I could imagine how the processes of fragmentation, isolation, and dissociation worked, and I could even spot them in stories my friends told me. But these were things other people experienced, not me. Maybe I'd experience them someday if something traumatic ever happened to me.

Solomon helped me understand that these ways of coping with trauma can happen in big, extreme ways—as they do in victims of PTSD—or in incredibly subtle ways and that I had experienced all of them. He also helped me see that symptoms often build up quietly over time until something breaks. And the origins of complex trauma are not a single event but are cumulative and environmental.

My breakup with Aspen was the catalyst that broke open an entire lifetime of being told in subtle and not so subtle ways that I wasn't worthy of love, care, or belonging. All those feelings came crashing into me with such force that I often couldn't get out of bed all day. This was not depression. It was profound pain. This kind of pain in my life had never had a place to go before because it had been invalidated by the religious, family, and community systems I was part of.

As I came to terms with what Solomon was helping me see for the first time, I began to understand how right he was. I had a long way to go in understanding the ways in which I'd been a victim of abuses before I could help others.

Trust

By late in my second year of grad school, my life had changed irreversibly. I had run far from the world in which I'd grown up but hadn't fully separated from it. I had spent countless hours reading, discussing, and trying to make sense of what I had been taught about God and the Bible. And I had decided to look for a faith that didn't have bigotry, racism, and shame built into its very soul. But the biggest transformation in my life came when the fallout from my breakup forced me to look directly at what I had been trying to resolve when I set out on my postcollege journey: I was struggling to cope with my pain.

Solomon gently helped me understand that for weeks in our discussions, I'd focused on the breakup because it was easier than looking at pain I had stuffed down and ignored over a lifetime. The breakup had lanced an abscess, and all the pus, blood, and infection built up over years of trying to exist within a toxic system were pouring out.

For more than twenty years, I had no one I could turn to for help, no one to say something like, "Hey, Matthias, it looks like behind that smile you're in a lot of pain. I wonder if you'd want to tell me about it?"

Well, that's not strictly true. I know some people tried to help me, but I scoffed. In effect, I told anyone who got close to asking me about my pain that they had no idea what they were talking about. I was doing just fine, thank you very much.

When in the past I'd shared my pain with the people closest to me, the ones who were supposed to care, I watched their faces turn to stone. They threw their God at me, and I understood that revealing myself wasn't safe. And I wasn't about to risk that anymore; I knew better.

This highlights what I think is one of the most difficult paradoxes of a runaway's journey. We set out to find something different and better, a place where we can rest, where we can be cared for and care for others. But receiving and learning how to rest in that care is incredibly difficult, and sometimes impossible, when we've experienced trauma.

Good care often exposes the places in our lives that haven't been tended. Our wounds sometimes hurt more after they receive attention because that care shows us a different reality is possible, one in which we don't have to shoulder our hurt alone.

Trusting someone who is trying to care for us can be difficult. We know with our whole bodies what it feels like to place our trust in someone who seems kind and loving, only to have them stab us when we least expect it. We don't want to risk that again. If this explanation resonates with you, please know that it's natural to be suspicious of care while simultaneously yearning for it.

You might wonder how I was able to trust Solomon enough to allow him to care for me. The truth is I had already spent a couple of years establishing trust with him, so when my heartbreak hit, I knew I could share it with Solomon instead of keeping it all inside. Because we had built a relationship of trust, together we could also start to access the well of pain underneath my loss. I could start to share other stories of deep hurt.

Solomon didn't brush me off. He sat with me in the pain, helping me stitch together the pieces of my broken heart.

Risk

A lot of people assume that those of us who are working in trauma-recovery fields have life figured out. We have dedicated years to studying trauma and human psychology, learning how to help people put the pieces of their lives back together, so surely we're somehow immune from becoming victims of abuse and trauma ourselves.

I believed this about myself when I was in grad school working on my counseling degree. I figured if I ever ended up in a situation where I was about to get hurt again, I would be able to spot it quickly and do all the right things to make sure everyone involved walked away unscathed. That's one of the perks of being an expert, right?

Surprise—reality is much messier.

It doesn't matter how much we "know." We can learn about trauma, systems of abuse, and how to heal. We can attend trainings and graduate school and get licenses and fancy certifications. None of those things will protect us.

Knowledge can help *explain* what happened to us, providing language to talk about and understand how brains react when trauma occurs. I don't want to dismiss the power of knowledge, but understanding isn't healing. If you're a runaway, you know this instinctively.

Almost any time I'm on Instagram, I see someone who has been deeply hurt by their faith explaining a system of abuse, often in an insightful, helpful way. Sometimes, it's clear that those posts are born of profound, unhealed pain. That's not a critique, just an observation. Understanding our trauma does not mean we have healed from our trauma.

I sometimes imagine what it would be like if I could somehow magically wave a wand and heal our trauma, yours and my own. This wand would apply a healing balm to our hearts, stitching up all the pain we hold, making what prompted our runaway journeys hurt far less. The wand wouldn't erase the pain because healing isn't erasure, but it would help us feel whole again. We'd have personhood and ground to stand on so we could move through the world with a renewed sense of security.

Let's say I wave this wand now—and poof! Just like that, we are healed.

What haunts me as I imagine this possibility is that *although you and I are healed, the systems that produced our pain still exist.*

Violence is still perpetrated daily. If we ourselves heal the moment my wand slices through the air, nothing guarantees we won't experience trauma again—possibly in the next moment.

The pervasive *systems* that produce and perpetuate trauma scare me and must be addressed.

Whistleblowers

We all know we live in a world of violence. And it seems to be getting progressively worse. Where is the evidence that Jesus's death and resurrection, his message of love and forgiveness, created a change in space and time? Why do we keep grasping at faith when much of the violence in the world comes from faith systems and even from our own families? Why would those of us who have been abused and traumatized within these systems look toward the very thing that is responsible for our pain?

In the past few years, I've moved from asking the question "Why bother with God or faith?" to asking "Why are you and I on this runaway journey anyway, fleeing God and faith and home?"

For me, questions about abuse, trauma, violence, scapegoating, and pain are the most compelling aspects of the story of Jesus. And I believe we can answer some of these questions if we take what Girard and Alison say seriously. I don't mean that we will arrive at certainty or explain why so many bad things happen in the world, but we may gain real hope.

Please know I'm not talking about an escapist hope or about pure optimism—just the opposite. I'm far from optimistic about what is going to happen in the next decade or century, but in the rest of this chapter, I'll try to explain what I mean by "real hope."

When we turn toward Jesus, we are turning toward a victim. A victim who *tells the truth* about what happened to him. A victim who exposes the reality of the violence he suffered. A victim who, throughout his teachings, compares himself with many other victims, including marginalized people who have suffered at the hands of the powerful and people who have been cast out and cast aside.

Jesus tells his followers that any time they see someone hungry or thirsty, a stranger, someone in need of clothing, someone who is sick or in prison, what his followers do or don't do for any of those people is what they are doing or not doing to Jesus himself.[1]

Jesus is revealing what James Alison calls "the intelligence of the victim."[2] The reality is that people at the edges or on the outside of *any* system can and do tell the truth about what is actually happening in that system. They can expose truth, like whistleblowers. Their intelligence and courage then become threatening to those in power, who use any means necessary to cast the truth-tellers out and put the blame on them in order to maintain power and a semblance of peace.

We've seen this before. It's called scapegoating.

Jesus equates himself with every victim of corrupt, brutal, dangerous systems by saying the way we treat other victims reflects how we treat him. When we scapegoat others, we scapegoat Jesus. When we exclude others, we exclude him. When we care for others, especially those we don't want to care for, we care for him. And when we listen to others, especially those in pain and those who reveal the ways they have suffered at the hands of human systems of violence, we listen to him.

Let's consider how revolutionary Jesus's declaration of himself as a victim was. Think about the arc of human history for a moment. How often do victims get to tell the story of what happened to them? "History is written by the victors, not the victims." We've already encountered that adage, haven't we?

Maybe a better question is: How often do we *listen* to what the victims are revealing? Marginalized people are always speaking, always telling the truth about the systems in which they struggle to survive, but speaking up usually gets them into a bigger mess—and often gets them killed.

Here's where my hope kicks in: I told you in the previous section that I believe we human beings are getting better at listening to victims. I believe that's happening because we're getting better at realizing that the people we scapegoat aren't evil but are members of our human family who are suffering at our own hands.

I see evidence that the seeds of what Jesus planted through his resurrection are growing in the midst of many systems that are no longer working. Clearly, we have a long way to go, but we are living in a world where more and more long-buried stories are being uncovered. The pen that writes our history is now in other hands, and the truth about what happened in the distant and recent past is being unearthed and shared.

More people are finding space to speak up and say, "This is my experience. This is how I'm hurting." And many more people are listening to these stories. In the same breath, many other people are pushing back *hard* against these stories, against the truth-telling by the people on the margins, again showing how powerful the systems of violence are and what is at stake. For example, transgender people are over four times more likely than cisgender people to be victims of violent crime.[3] While many trans and queer activists continue to sound the alarm, advocating for policy change and protections, many other people refuse to acknowledge the lived realities of transgender people, denying their very existence, and pushing to enact antitrans legislation that further endangers their lives.[4]

Who do we listen to? The people who are telling us about their pain, or those who deny it exists? This is a question of empathy. It's question of sympathy and compassion that is strong enough to fracture walls. As we investigate whose stories we're listening to, we learn more about the lies and harm that are yet to be undone, a world full of harm. But I believe we will continue to see the ripple effects of all Jesus invited us to hear, see, and do by listening to those who we have marginalized and allowing those walls to crack and crumble. Instead of fleeing to dogma and rigid definitions of Truth, we can turn toward that warm breeze of empathy and let it transform us. This is the invitation of Jesus.

Alison describes what happens once we begin to realize that we are scapegoating innocent people: "It makes it impossible for us really to bring about *with a good conscience* any of the sacred resolutions, the sacrificial decisions which brought us, and bring all societies, comparative peace and order. The game is up. And so human desire, rivalry, and competition, which had previously been kept in some sort of check by a system of prohibitions, rituals, sacrifices and myths, lest human groups collapse in perpetual and irresolvable mutual vengeance, can no longer be controlled in this way."[5]

In other words, because we have been shown the inner workings of our systems of violence, we now know what we are doing when we scapegoat others. We're casting out, hurting, excluding, and murdering *someone who is just like us.*

"Let's seal off the borders from people like us. Let's brutalize and demonize people like us." That just doesn't pack the right punch, does it?

When we fully understand our scapegoats are no different from us, we can't reinforce systems of violence or bring peace by justifying exclusion. A current-day example of this is how attitudes have shifted around LGBTQ+ inclusion in many spaces.

What happens instead? At first, more fracturing as the system is exposed for what it is: meaningless violence. The powerful people who try to attribute meaning to their violence by naming it as "sacred" lose their power when everyone sees what's happening. We see how the creation of victims serves the purpose of shoring up all the systems of power and control—and as soon as that happens, the systems stop working.

Repentance

As runaways, we are involved in the changes Alison describes when he says "the game is up." I'd like to now look at how our religious and sacred systems work and what happens when we run from them.

We know that our systems have declared certain individuals and groups of people "bad" or "evil." We runaways have listened to those people, hearing their pain, and realized they're neither bad nor evil; they're like us.

If you're among the groups labeled evil, you've probably already awakened to the pain of being scapegoated. Perhaps you've asked or even begged the people doing the scapegoating to see you for who you truly are and to feel empathy.

The more we listen to victims, Alison explains, the more the systems of violence that create victims break down. Everything tends to stop working when the truth about systemic violence is out in the open. As a collective—but not always as individuals—we know the stories people in power tell us often aren't true. There's always more than one story, but justifications for violence and exclusion rarely allow for more than one story, making them woefully inadequate.

This happened on a large scale in the United States in the summer of 2020 after the murders of George Floyd and Breonna Taylor. The truth of their innocence was impossible for the collective to ignore, causing thousands of people to take to the streets in response to continued police violence. The system began to crack because the truth was being told; this caused *more* unrest and *more* violence by those who were invested in maintaining the systems of violence. While the system didn't break entirely that summer, the cracks are far bigger than they were before.

Groups of people—large and small—count on scapegoating and rallying around the exclusion of "others" to create peace, but that's failing more and more often today. Peace based on exclusion and prejudice is no longer as easy to grasp, but unfortunately, that means there is less peace in the world, not more. As the myth of peace upheld at the expense of others falls apart, those in power are threatened because their primary means of retaining power no longer works.

Cheryl A. Kirk-Duggan, a womanist theologian who studies violence, explains, "For the model to work, violence must always be directed against those who cannot or will not fight back because the group will disintegrate into murderous rivalry: intense, destructive competition among themselves."[1]

I believe we are witnessing a form of that disintegration happening among Americans today as the culture of white supremacy enforced in part by police brutality is being exposed. We're also witnessing it in religious and faith communities as those who have historically been excluded are stepping up and naming the violence they've been subjected to, people like us runaways.

What choice remains for the powerful people who define themselves over and against others?

They could continue the cycle of violence by doubling down—increasing violent attacks, setting up more rules and prohibitions, or finding another scapegoat. This is often the default choice, the choice that feels like good religion because it allows people to fall back upon their sacred systems of over-and-against identity.

Or they could listen to the marginalized and less powerful and learn the truth. In short, they could look honestly at what they have done, confess, and *repent.*

Repent is a word freighted with all kinds of meanings for those of us in religious and sacred systems. So what do I mean by it?

Repentance is *acknowledging sincerely* what you have done and *committing sincerely* to changing directions. You're stopping in your tracks, turning, and looking at the one you previously turned your back on to make that commitment.

It's easy to point a finger at every person we wish would repent, every single person we've watched double down on violence instead of changing course. But as we do that, we also need to see the interconnections of our actions—the way pointing our finger sets us up to fall back into creating meaning that is over and against others. Aren't we again making ourselves the good guys who can repent while the other person becomes the bad guy who won't repent?

In the same way, when we look at others and easily recognize where they need to repent, we have to be able to turn that eye upon ourselves, especially those of us who are privileged by society. Dr. Kirk-Duggan cautions, "Before you answer 'I am not prejudiced,' ask yourself: 'Who are my friends?' 'Whom do I associate with?' 'Whom do I tend to blame, be suspicious of, or ignore just by the way they look and move?'"[2] She continues, "To deny the existence of our own biases is to engage a pathology in which we actually escalate our behavioral prejudices."[3]

As pastor Nadia Bolz-Weber often says, "Our drug of choice right now is knowing who we're better than."[4] And we're super good at mainlining that drug whether explicitly by pointing fingers or implicitly in the ways Dr. Kirk-Duggan is describing.

In the twenty-first century, we're watching systems of violence fall apart as victims speak out on a grand scale. As I said earlier, when violent systems fall apart, that leads to *more* violence instead of less, at least initially. Basically, things get worse before they get better. Girard told us we should expect that.

One way of reading Jesus's own words in Matthew 24 supports this idea as well. He famously says, "You will hear of wars and rumors of wars but see to it that you are not alarmed. Such things must happen, but the end is still to come. Nation will rise against nation, and kingdom against kingdom. There will be famines and earthquakes in various places. All these are the beginning of birth pains."[5]

Ours is a world full of wars and rumors of wars, where things are falling apart, but also a world where something new and better is being born out of the pain.

Inconvenient

Because of what Jesus revealed to us about ourselves, we can answer some important questions:

First, we can answer questions about the meaning of "sacred" or "redemptive" violence, the idea baked into some branches of Christianity that God sends us suffering to test us or to purify us, that suffering is God's will, or perhaps that God is responsible for the violence toward people we don't like. In this way of thinking, God unleashes violence—in the form of floods, hurricanes, wars, and any number of other things—to punish people.

But we can say confidently that these things are not of God.

Instead, they are projections of natural and human violence on to God. These are our ideas of what we think a God should be, what we want a God to be. We want a God who shows the bad people who is right. And, of course, we want to be the good people.

But as we've already discussed, violence has nothing to do with God. I now view the Bible as a book that shows us all the ways humans have blamed God for our own murderousness and cruelty and how we have gradually discovered that God has nothing to do with our violence. Biblical scholar Wilda Gafney wrestles with this saying: "The scriptures teach we are made in the image of God while offering a God who sometimes seems to be made in the image of humanity, showcasing all the worst parts."[1] She explains there is incredible violence in the Scriptures and that Jesus uses language of slavery without a second thought. Yet instead of finding this as cause to throw Scripture out, she writes that it calls us "to listen, read, and hear deeply, what the Spirit is saying to her people."[2] These things are an invitation to look closer.

So let's look closer at the question of God's character. If God is *not* a God of violence, then maybe we can more fully embrace God as nothing but love.

This theme seems to be carried throughout Scripture, "God is Love."[3]

And then there are Jesus's first and second commandments: Love God. And love your neighbor as you love yourself.[4]

Do you see how inconvenient, to put it mildly, those words are? In those few words, Jesus completely undoes the violence in myriad religious systems. And to further complicate things, Jesus seems to suggest in some Gospels that our "neighbor" is anyone we encounter, and thus his commandment undoes the creation of the "in" and "out" groups on which all our systems depend by essentially telling us there is no distinction. We are all in the same group—our neighbors and ourselves. We are profoundly interconnected.

Jesus's commandment about treating others like we treat ourselves is hard. It's linked to the question of how we undo systems of violence built on treating others as different from ourselves. So how do we accomplish this dismantling of violence?

Are you ready?

We undo systems of violence by loving our neighbors as we love ourselves.

Before you roll your eyes and dismiss me as a weak-ass, tone-deaf flower child telling everyone, "We just gotta all love each other, bro," give me a chance to tell you what I mean by *love*.

Love

I had been hearing my friend Rachael Clinton Chen talk for years about how she felt she was finally getting the chance to step into a pastoral role after a lifetime of being told she wasn't qualified because of her gender. She told me the reality was different from how she imagined, but I had no doubt it was the perfect role for her. I saw her eyes sparkle as she talked about what it was like to be at the front of a room teaching and sharing. We both sensed she was stepping into something she was made for.

The first time I saw Rachael teach, I was sitting in the back of a large room. She took the stage, and as she began talking, something new started happening—the energy in the room settled. It's something that has happened almost every time I've seen her teach since then. When there's something a bit frenetic in the air, the usual buzz of a big crowd of people, it always calms as she talks.

Rachael doesn't fit the conventional description of a talented speaker. She's not loud, nor is she flashy, nor is she the most organized. She tells stories and shows up however she is, and it always works.

On the first day I watched her, she was agitated and distracted, and she just told us the truth: "I'm agitated and distracted right now, but let's see if we can get through this together." She then shared some of the experiences of spiritual abuse she had to wrestle with growing up as a woman in the southern Baptist world.

As she spoke, I looked around and noticed people in the room were entirely engrossed in her stories. Many were tearing up. I felt my own sadness rise to the surface as she gently but honestly shared her story. She didn't shy away from calling what she had experienced exactly what it was: abuse.

In the midst of her talk, Rachael said something about love. She offered a definition from our colleague, a trauma therapist named Abby Wong-Heffter, based on Abby's work with countless survivors of abuse and harm. Abby believes love is the presence of "attunement, containment, and repair."

We've already explored attunement, way back at the beginning of this book. Remember how the parents in the still-face experiment were fully attuned to their babies' needs and emotions at the start? Attunement is a form of presence but not just presence. It's *presence with intention.* Neuroscientist Daniel Siegel describes attunement as "feeling felt" when with another person.[1]

Rachael offered a definition of containment, saying it's like attunement but is someone's ability to "hold" what is happening to another in the moment without becoming dysregulated too. Think of the parent of a child who is having a temper tantrum. The parent may be able to attune to the child's anger and then describe to that child what they are experiencing without joining them in their dysregulation.

"It seems like you are so angry right now," the parent might say. That is providing containment.

Or think about the last time you went to someone to have a difficult conversation. Did that person lash out at you? Or were they able to listen and stay present with you? Were they able to consider the possibility that they might have done something wrong, or did they place all the blame back on you? The ability to contain is the ability to stay regulated in the presence of another person, creating space for their experience without shutting them down.

Rachael explained that *repair is what emerges out of attunement and containment.* In any relationship, things are going to go wrong. That is inevitable and should be expected. Psychologists call this *rupture*, and it's a vital part of human relationships, so much so that many relationship experts claim that if you're not experiencing rupture in your relationships, it means someone isn't actually showing up. Someone's not actually being real.

It's not that the rupture itself isn't important, but what's even more important is how we deal with that rupture. When rupture happens, is there repair? Is someone able to apologize for what they did wrong? Or is there further fracturing? Attunement and containment are vital steps in repairing relationships when rupture happens. And, as Rachael explained, the ability to repair *within* relationships is how trust is built.

As she defined attunement, containment, and repair, something clicked for me in a powerful way. These weren't new categories for me; they're pretty basic components of how many therapists frame healthy relationships. But I'd never heard them grouped together in this way, nor had I heard them defined as "love" before. I looked around the room and would swear I saw light bulbs going off above other people's heads too. It explained so much!

Rachael's framing of these aspects of love explained why I felt so empty within churches and communities that would exclaim, "Love the sinner but hate the sin!" Attunement to the pain I was experiencing had been nonexistent. Containment? Nope, I was an abomination. Repair? They couldn't even begin to hear me through their useless platitudes.

That wasn't love. It was a concrete box.

As Yourself

As I sat with Abby and Rachael's definition of love, it became clearer and clearer to me that Rachael wasn't describing something weak or without power but something incredibly strong.

When Jesus says, "Love your neighbor as yourself," maybe he's inviting us into an ongoing process of attuning, containing, and repairing with our neighbor. And remember, a neighbor is anyone we come into contact with.

But what about that other part, the "as yourself" part?

As I sat in my therapist's office processing through my own difficult breakup and the lifetime of pain it had unearthed, my understanding of Jesus's words deepened. I didn't know it, but I hadn't attuned to my own pain. My own pain wasn't contained. It certainly hadn't been repaired.

I had fractured, isolated, and dissociated.

For the first time in my life, I felt disparate pieces of myself coming together in an environment where someone else—in this case, Solomon—could love me. Maybe that sounds like a strange thing to say about my therapist, but there are several studies showing that one of the largest indicators of therapeutic "success" is not the methodology used but the therapist's love for their client.[1] Solomon had helped me build my own ability to attune, contain, and repair myself. And in turn, I was going to be able to offer that to others who needed that kind of love.

As I began to heal, I was able to venture into other people's pain more fully. Remember the maxim from The Seattle School? As a therapist, I could only go as far as I had been myself, and now I was able to go so much further.

Another way of putting it is the line RuPaul says at the end of every episode of *Drag Race:* "If you can't love yourself, how the hell you gonna love anybody else?"

But what Ru doesn't say is the flipside, which is equally as true: "How can you love if you haven't been loved yourself?"

We love because we have been loved. And so many of us haven't been loved well because we've been stuck in profoundly violent systems. As a result, we haven't been able to love others—our neighbors—well.

That's what I believe Jesus came to show us. By choosing to be the victim of a violent system and carrying the results to full completion in death. Like the apostle Paul writes, "The wages of sin is death."[2] The result of a violent system of who's in and who's out, creating scapegoats to reaffirm our own goodness and identity, the result of that kind of structuring is always death.

But in Jesus's case, death doesn't have the final say, and violence doesn't have the final say. Jesus subverted death and showed us all there's a much bigger reality at work, the reality of love. This reality of love can only be learned by loving the victim, the weak, the outcasts, the scapegoats.

The moment we start loving the victims, the moment we start attuning to, containing, and attempting to repair with the victims of our systems' violence, is the moment the entire system begins to shatter.

That's the moment the concrete irrevocably breaks.

Complicity

None of the changes we're talking about are easy. It's difficult to shift attention away from ourselves toward others while also acknowledging that we can only turn to the other's pain successfully if we have first tuned in to our own.

A few years ago, a friend told me that one of the best ways to get an education in what it means to be white and privileged in the United States is to follow hundreds of people on social media who are different from you. I took that message to heart, and I think they were right. I followed Black people. I followed disabled people. I followed trans people.

"Don't interact," my friend told me. "Don't do anything that even remotely brings your presence into the equation. Just observe. For years."

This may not be the best advice for you, but I can tell you it's been eye-opening for me. I *often* run across ideas and concepts that piss me off or make me roll my eyes or say to my screen, "You're such an idiot." But I keep listening and trying to understand why I'm having that reaction.

For example, right now it's happening for me around ability. I see someone on social media complaining about not being able to access a space, and my initial reaction is almost always annoyance. It takes a lot of work for me to get to a place of wondering, *Maybe this person isn't complaining but instead is sharing their experience and how much it hurts.*

It takes even more work to wonder what it would be like to not be able to access a place everyone you know can go easily. There's a relatively jaded part of me that gets very loud first and says, "Maybe you just need to accept that some spaces aren't for you. Be grateful for what you have."

That's not attunement. Not containment. Not repair.

But it's a common response. In an essay sharing her experiences as a disabled Black woman riding New York City's paratransit service for disabled people, Britney Wilson writes that it's ubiquitous for people to view her and other disabled people as entitled when they share their experiences: "It's the idea that we are acting as if someone owes us something rather than merely asking to be treated with the respect and human dignity we deserve. It's the belief that people of a certain status or apparent condition have no right to demand better because we should just be happy with whatever we get. We should be happy we have anything at all."[1]

I know that feeling Britney is describing within myself.

That feeling is combative and fracturing. It's an indicator that there's something inside me I haven't looked at and worked through—probably some of my own pain from when I wasn't able to access certain spaces. Of course, the pain occurred in a different way, but the buttons that set it off were similar.

If—and let's be clear, it's a big *if*—I can become curious about my initial response instead of rolling my eyes and continuing to scroll, if I can start to wonder what's underneath my reaction, I will again face a lot of pain—someone else's pain and my own pain. Both will probably be profound pain. Pain that will make me want to weep and will require that I face the injustice of this world and its systems of violence head on.

I will also have to face the fact that I participate in these systems of violence. In this case, I'm participating in the systems of ableism.

I don't like this process. I'm not good at this.

If I were to overlay Abby and Rachael's definition of love on this experience, it gets worse for me. My initial reaction to so many people sharing their pain is far from attunement. It's the opposite; it's dismissal. If I were to attune, it would mean I'd need to truly feel the impact of their words, and that would mean I had to work with every reaction that came up within me. All my defensiveness, all my anger ("Why on earth do I get angry at people sharing their pain?") I'd need to contain. If I were somehow able to do all of that, I'd then have to acknowledge that I am complicit in a system that harms disabled people day in and day out.

Again, I don't like this.

But that's not even the hardest part. Next comes the process of repair. And in this case, that means repenting for my own complicity and then *doing something about it*. And if you're wondering, that does not mean sending a reply to someone saying, "I'm so sorry you couldn't access that space. That's awful!"

Repair would mean I'd have to take a hard look at the ways I live my life in an ableist manner and do everything I could to change those ways.

Even as I write this, I feel my body squirm and my stomach drop. I'm not against doing any of the things I've outlined above. But I'm getting honest about how little I'm doing at this moment. I'm barely living up to what I would tell you is a true conviction of mine.

What constitutes "repair" is not something that I get to define. None of these things is rightfully defined by me. The people who are most harmed get to create the definitions. The actual disabled people in my life are the ones who get to tell me, "Matthias, you're not hearing me" or "What you did there wasn't actually helpful."

Love means I cannot stay complicit after I hear someone who has been harmed by systems of violence share their experience. Anything less is not love. The apostle James echoes this notion when he writes, "Do not merely listen to the word, and so deceive yourselves. Do what it says. Anyone who listens to the word but does not do what it says is like someone who looks at his face in the mirror and, after looking at himself, goes away and immediately forgets what he looks like."[2]

What is the "word" James is talking about? He's referring to Jesus's word. And what has Jesus revealed? He has showed us what it means to listen to a victim of a violent system. If we hold these things together, could James be challenging us to listen to those who are oppressed?

If we just listen without action, we can easily get pulled into the deception of self-righteousness. Remember when we all put black boxes on our social media pages after George Floyd was murdered by police instead of doing something about police violence? That was not love. Nor was it merely self-righteousness. It was the perpetuation of violence. Community organizer and activist Pascale Diverlus writes that #BlackoutTuesday "felt like one, big, painful slap in the face. After all, we've seen the same pattern again and again: A tragic event takes place, non-Black people feign shock, release empty statements, make donations, and maybe *maybe* post some resources and then they're right back to radio silence."[3] I would argue this was among the worst kinds of violence because we said, "I see you. I'm listening to you. I see you are hurting. And now I'm not going to do anything about it."

Actual love would require us to suffer, to actually give up our own lives for the sake of another. It would require us to give up the comfort of the privileges of the life we hold and work to repair the system of white supremacy in which we are complicit.

Or, as the apostle John writes, "There is no greater love than to lay down one's life for one's friends."[4]

We can't say we love someone without being willing to give up the life we know for their sake. I think any of us who has had a taste of being marginalized knows what it's like to have someone claim friendship with us as a form of clout. I have several nonaffirming pastor friends who have used their relationship with me as some sort of proof that they love LGBTQ+ people, and we've had some conversations about why this is a problem.

For love to be present, the pastors would have to be willing to lay down their entire livelihood, the lives they know as pastors of conservative churches, to lay all that down in order to undo the harm done by the system of violence they're perpetrating even as they call me a friend.

Judged

While the apostle James seems to denounce listening to a victim without doing anything to help, Jesus says something similar but with a surprising twist: "If anyone hears my words but does not keep them, I do not judge that person. For I did not come to judge the world, but to save the world."[1]

Save the world from what?

If you're tracking with me up until this point, we can confidently answer: Jesus, the victim of horrific, bloody human violence, came to save the world from that human violence.

I believe Jesus is getting at something that makes the reality of love—of listening to and loving victims of our systems— even harder. Jesus is naming the truth: We will fail in love. And yet, as he says, there is no judgment in his declaration. In fact, he understands that our failure is what makes us human.

In declaring he doesn't come to judge us, Jesus is highlighting our own propensity to judge—and to cast our judgment upon the divine. A lot of people use this biblical passage for the purpose of confirming that God is judgmental because the very next thing Jesus says is dire: "There is a judge for the one who rejects me and does not accept my words; the very words I have spoken will condemn them at the last day. For I did not speak on my own, but the Father who sent me commanded me to say all that I have spoken. I know that his command leads to eternal life. So, whatever I say is just what the Father has told me to say."[2]

Cue all your projections of what this condemnation at the last day means. You're probably thinking that means Jesus might not judge you now, but God is surely going to condemn you in the end.

But Jesus says, "The very words I have spoken will condemn them," not that God is the one who judges, but the words themselves judge. Or, alternatively, the stories themselves do the judging. I wonder if Jesus is suggesting that on the "last day" (whatever that means), all stories will be revealed, all systems will be stripped bare. By extension, I believe he's saying that the reality of our own participation in violence will become inescapable, and we will have to look in the face all those we have harmed—and we will look in the face of Jesus.

Could it be that Jesus is referring to words he uttered while experiencing such profound violence at the hands of a religious and political system?

"Father, forgive them, for they do not know what they are doing."?[3]

Could it be that when he talks about condemnation, Jesus is not referring to judgment but instead is referring to the revelation of the full knowledge of what we have done? Coupled with the assertion that our deeds are not being held against us but are forgiven. The black hole of violent retaliation is filled through love.

A good psychological definition of forgiveness is a "conscious, deliberate decision to release feelings of resentment or vengeance toward a person or group who has harmed you."[4] But that definition doesn't do it justice. If you've ever had the experience of someone forgiving you for something horrible you've done, you know it's an unnerving experience. That moment of realization and approaching someone you've hurt is agonizing. The work of naming the harm you've caused and apologizing for it is never easy. And when someone says, "I forgive you," it's the strangest mix of relief and awe.

But forgiveness doesn't mean that the harmful consequences of your actions just go away.

On the other side is the experience of someone coming to you *asking* for forgiveness. You may remember a time when someone harmed you, and they knew they had harmed you. They were able to put into words what they did wrong, and it was clear they knew the impact their actions had on you. You got the kind of apology by which you felt heard and seen, so you almost couldn't help but say, "Thank you. I forgive you."

Attunement. Containment. Repair.

I wonder if this is what Jesus was talking about: A reckoning with harm that is self-evident because the people who have been harmed are inescapable, right in front of us. Their very words convict and condemn.

But instead of being met with vengeance and violence, there is enough containment that people are able to move to grief. Otherwise known as repentance. They're able to recognize their harm and name it, apologize for it, do something about it. Genuinely, not from a place of shame but from a place of conviction. And change directions.

This kind of thing would take time, wouldn't it? In order for it to be real, it couldn't happen instantaneously. It would have to be worked out gradually over time.

Now say there's an entire system on the line, an entire system that is built on violence and scapegoating. For that system to be undone, it would take years, wouldn't it? Maybe even millennia?

It also would mean that we're essentially all in the same boat. And maybe this is what Jesus is getting at when he says, "If anyone hears my words but does not keep them, I don't judge them." He's talking about all of us—every human who hears a story of harm and dismisses it.

It's also human to hear those stories, try to do something about our own complicity, and then look at others who aren't willing to look at their complicity and judge them. It's easy to fall back into systems of violence as we attempt to escape violence.

It's easy to rebuild the walls around our own self-righteousness. The very walls we have been trying to escape.

But Jesus is revealing that this, too, is human. It's what he's here to save us from. We're all in the same boat, all part of the same system of violence, all being invited into a larger reality that takes pain seriously, a system that moves toward repair because its very nature is love.

A new reality that is slowly being born, birthed within the old violent one.

Part 7

Faith

It Is Well

Growing up, my school friends thought the church my family went to was primitive because we didn't have a worship team and banks of high-tech audiovisual equipment hidden behind a curtain. No fancy big screen projecting images of waterfalls and sunsets, highlighting the words of a worship song everyone already knew from listening to the local Christian radio station.

We just had a shiny polished walnut grand piano. And a blue paper hymnal we had to dig out from under the chairs in front of us.

"Turn to Hymn 705," Paul, our worship leader, would say, standing on what was more like a step than a stage. "Hymn 705, 'It Is Well with My Soul,'" he would repeat, giving us time to flip through the pages. It was never enough time.

"Hymn 705," Paul would repeat a third time and, without taking a breath, launch into the first verse: "When peace like a river attendeth my way . . ."

I always looked toward the piano, eager to see flashes of strong, pale hands flying over the keys. We didn't need waterfalls and sunsets. We had Elaine, who had spent time in some of the finest concert halls in the country. She didn't play any of the notes on the page but filled the cavernous space of the church with a perfect melody.

The women in the congregation sang, "It is well," followed by the deep bass of the men echoing, "It is well." My voice wasn't deep, so I sang with the women—when I wasn't completely entranced by the piano.

I was sure this was what heaven would sound like.

I remember Sundays as joyful—dressing up, laughing with friends, playing hide-and-seek in the giant church basement with my sisters, and driving forty-five minutes to Des Moines for lunch at a restaurant. We didn't have a lot of money for eating out, but my dad didn't think my mom should have to cook on Sundays. For Sunday supper, it was popcorn—always popcorn—paired with movies we watched together as a family, followed by smoothies and apples and cheese.

When I think about home and my childhood faith, these memories are some of the first and best that come to mind.

But with those happy memories come memories of self-doubt, pain, and loss.

I remember furiously whispering confessions to God right before taking communion. As young as age eight or nine, I knew if I didn't confess enough, if I didn't remember all the ways I had sinned since the last time we took communion, I would drop dead right as I put the bread in my mouth.

It wasn't dying that terrified me; it was the fact that everybody around me would *know*. They'd know something was wrong with me, that I'd done something so bad that God needed to smite me then and there. I knew the moment my body hit the floor, they'd all know that the crushes and puppy love my friends felt for girls in my class I was feeling for boys.

Every communion, my face blanched with fear, my stomach twisted, and my limbs tightened as I searched my memory for the last hint of "sin" to silently confess.

On Sundays in that little Iowa church, the joy I experienced with God, my family, and the sound of sacred music was forever linked to terror and shame in the flesh of my body.

Still I kept singing, "It is well."

Alone

Remember that annoyingly accurate part of Brené Brown's *The Gifts of Imperfection*? The part where she says the only thing that separates someone with a strong sense of love and belonging from someone who doesn't have that sense is their belief in their own worthiness.

I think I really understand what she means now. And I think I may also understand what Jesus means when he says we only need a teeny tiny speck of faith to move mountains.

I used to read Brené Brown's and Jesus's wise words (*are* they the same person? We'll never know) and think all the responsibility was on me. I imagined a real tug-of-war where I was on one end of the rope and faith and worthiness were on the other end. All I had to do was pull them over to my side, and I'd win.

I've also played that tug-of-war game with my parents, with my church communities, with the people I called my friends, and with the theology I once believed in. If I could just be a little stronger, my faith would be so obvious and so powerful. Mountains would move. Everyone would praise my worthiness.

I'd hear the voice of God saying, "Well done, Matthias! Well done!"

But I've finally learned that faith and worthiness are not games of strength.

A couple of years after my big breakup, I was talking with Solomon when he said, "I think we keep bumping into something deep—a place you're not able to go. Do you feel that too?"

I admitted I did. And I had been feeling it for a while. Sometimes in the middle of a session with Solomon I would feel my stomach knot and my hands clench tight. The resistance within me would become urgent and powerful, and I would redirect the conversation or just flat out say, "Let's stop. I don't want to explore that now."

These moments of resistance happened when Solomon tried to connect something I was experiencing in my current life with something from my past.

Finally, when he asked, "Do you feel that too?" I knew we were thinking the same thing and whispered the answer.

"It's grief."

He nodded.

I immediately seized up, as usual. "I'm sorry, but I don't want to go there."

"Grief and sadness have never been safe for you, Matthias. You're going to need a lot of safety to be able to experience the deeper levels of grief you contain."

I thought for a moment and told him that part of the reason I was so resistant to going there with him was that we met for only fifty minutes in any given session. If I opened up one day, I would quickly be alone in my grief, and I was afraid of that.

I started to research options outside weekly therapy. I found another therapist, someone who specialized in daylong intensive work on grief, and brought the idea to Solomon. He approved.

"It might take us years to get to what you could access in a day with more safety and intention around you. I'm glad you're doing this," he told me.

Cut to a cold December day, when I walked into a room full of warm natural light with couches and comfy chairs and blankets spread around and began tapping into my well of grief. The therapist, whom I'll call Alice, gently led me through memories of my childhood, including what I loved about my parents. And there was so much I loved.

I remembered sitting in my room as a toddler after I'd been put to bed and hearing my dad play his harmonica. The bright, cheerful tones drifted through the whole house. I remembered laughing in the kitchen with my mom as she taught me how to grind wheat and make loaves of soft, warm bread.

Alice invited me to tap into how loved, cherished, and safe I felt in those moments.

I admit I was a bit suspicious at first. After all, I wasn't there to process the good things about my life. After resisting it for years, I was ready to grieve all the pain and loss.

And soon, that's what happened. Alice was guiding me through feelings of joy and love so I could then feel the depths of my sadness too.

Over the course of the day, we moved deeper into memories. I sat on the couch, wrapped in blankets, and we started to do work around the time when I came out to my parents.

I talked about how they treated me in those conversations and afterward, suddenly blurting out, "I just feel so alone, so abandoned."

"You are alone," Alice said with kindness and empathy in her eyes.

I began to weep.

Her words weren't meant to be cruel, just truthful. Their simplicity touched on something I had felt for so long but had never been able to admit, even to myself. I had tried for over a decade to get my childhood community to reopen their arms to me. And more important, I was still striving to get my parents to embrace me, to reassemble our family. I was still hoping that what felt like abandonment was only temporary.

Alice's simple words exposed the futility of all those hopes. I had been holding tight to my end of the rope, still thinking we were playing a game of tug-of-war and if I just gripped tighter and pulled harder, one day everyone would fly over to my side.

But no one was holding the other end of the rope. They never had been. Alice was right. I was alone.

Worthy

Alice and Solomon helped me see that for years I'd been pulling a rope with no one on the other end. And at the same time, I'd been pushing against immovable walls designed to keep me out.

All that pulling and pushing had only kept me trapped—bound by old fears and messages reinforcing the idea that I am not worthy. That my faith is not big enough. That I'm only as good as dirt. That I need to repent.

Another way to understand this would be through the language I learned about reflective desire. As I was pressing against the walls I was determined to break through, *my desire was still being shaped by those walls.*

I'd built my identity around being a runaway and an outsider, purposefully fleeing my community. But deep down, I believed I would one day be accepted as an insider again if I proved my worthiness, if I renewed and grew my faith.

Ever since I read Brené Brown's work on worthiness, I'd been on a quest to believe that I was worthy, to feel that I belonged somewhere again. But I think Brown left something out of her analysis—the thing that has become apparent to me only recently on my own journey. It's a truth I've attempted to share with you here: *Those who believe they are worthy have been shown they are worthy.*

Our belief in our worthiness reflects the system we live in. That system might be as small as a family or as large as a culture, but each system declares certain people are worthy and others are not.

In other words, we can't just will ourselves into believing in our own worthiness. Like any change in our bodies and minds, we have to learn and transform through experience. Worthiness is not just a belief but a full, embodied sense that we have a place in the world. This sense of belonging goes far beyond our cognitive mind. We experience it physically, like the sigh of relief when the final puzzle piece snaps into place.

Love is the same. We reflect the love we have received. We can only attune, contain, and repair for others to the extent that we have been attuned to, contained by, and repaired with by others.

We love because we have first been loved. We are beings who reflect our environments, and this truth is both tragic and hopeful.

I believe this truth about love is the core message of Jesus and is linked to what he tells us about that tiny mustard seed of faith. Like the disciples who hoped to heal a suffering child, Jesus invites us to participate in another system, another way of being outside our physical world of violence and pain. A place of pure, noncompetitive love. It's there for us if we have just the tiniest seed of faith. It doesn't take much.

We are made from love and made to be loved. And we know in our very bones that this world of violence and pain is not a place we can rest; it's not our home.

But love isn't easy. Love requires active participation, not under the fist of violence or retribution. With love, we can slowly learn to hear the stories of people we have hurt, either directly or indirectly, and apologize without taking on the burden of being bad or worthless.

Home is a place we can tell our own stories of pain and be met with love, apologies, and a commitment to a better world. It's a place where we can learn from our mistakes, not seeking perfection but justice. A place where the underdogs tell all their stories and where the powerful repent. It's a place where we get to be human. Because we are human.

Breeze

Let's go back to faith and parables for a moment.

What if, for us runaways, that tiny little mustard seed of faith amounts to just opening up our hands that have been gripping ropes so tightly and letting go?

What if dropping the rope allows us to refocus our attention on that warm, soft breeze that has been swirling around us all this time? The breeze I felt when I first poked my head beyond the walls that trapped me to find God was there too.

The breeze is whispering:

You already are loved.
You already belong.
You already are worthy.
You don't have to keep striving.

I felt the same breeze seeping through cracks in the walls, through windows and doors, repeating:

They already are loved.
They already belong.
They already are worthy.
They don't have to keep striving.

My faith now tells me that breeze is the breath of a God who looks nothing like what I thought God should look like.

This God doesn't recognize "in" groups and "out" groups and doesn't help buttress walls between people. This God invites us to take apart the ways we define and prove our worthiness.

This God, as Jesus told us, is love.

Perhaps it's the warm breath of God that makes us worthy.

Perhaps it's this breath that gives us life and identity, an identity that invites us to love because God has loved us first. Loved us with the kind of love that is toothsome, moving us into attunement, containment, and repair.

This kind of love also reminds us we still have capacity to do great harm when we get distracted by building walls to keep others out.

This kind of love assures us *our* pain is worthy of being listened to, attuned to, grieved over, fought for and then invites us to listen to others' pain.

This kind of love takes away our fears and replaces them with more faith, leading us again to a place where a warm breeze flows.

Friends

One of the most difficult characteristics of religious trauma is that it doesn't affect only our perceptions of ourselves or God or religion, but it also affects our perceptions and interactions with our communities. We become wary of whole groups of people because we know in our bodies that communities can cause deep harm, even in the name of love.

So we run away from churches, religions, and other people.

We bristle and are suspicious of any group that might repeat hurtful dynamics we've experienced in the past, even a group of ladies who like to get together on Tuesday nights to knit.

And yet as lovely as a cabin alone in the woods might sound, isolation isn't going to give us what we want. Part of being human is that we need community.

Before you go at me, let me be clear: I'm not saying we should all go back to church.

Let's look at the advice of Cheryl Kirk-Duggan, the womanist theologian we met in part 6, who studies violence. In her book *Refiner's Fire: A Religious Engagement with Violence*, Kirk-Duggan affirms profound trauma can come from communities, but we simply cannot escape our need for other people.

She proposes what she calls an *ekklesia*. That's the Greek word many New Testament writers use for "church." But Kirk-Duggan defines *ekklesia* as "a group of friends."[1] Specifically, it's a group of friends who engage oppressive systems and lean into the spiritual through relationships. "In doing so," she writes, "an *ekklesia* creates a sphere of justice, antithetical to the traditional patriarchal church. These experiences of grace allow for refining the fires of justice, imagination, and dialogue."[2]

We could also call this a group of friends who can be real about their pain with each other, including the pain of injustice and oppression. Friends who can then imagine and work toward a different reality together.

Can you recall a bad experience that's happened to you, something truly unjust? Now imagine that you went to a group of your best friends and told them about it.

If your friends are anything like mine, they would first listen and then get fired up. They'd attune to your pain and be upset on your behalf. But while holding the frustration and sadness, they'd also try to make it fun, to cheer you up. At some point in the evening, you might all end up laughing about what happened. Not in a way that erases the injustice but as a way of transforming it. And likely, you'd all come up with a plan to *do* something about it.

The kind of *ekklesia* I imagine includes friends who watch trashy TV one night and the next night stay up late over a glass of wine sharing their souls. Friends who reflect and affirm each other's worthiness and belonging, no matter what.

Another translation of the word *ekklesia* is "a gathering." Undoubtedly, this is where the student-led Sunday night chapel service at my college got its name. Remember that gathering where I wasn't allowed to speak out of fear of what it would do to the community? The gathering that deemed me unworthy.

I wonder what would happen if we gave up all that tethers us to old religious systems, churches, and harmful theology and just found a group of good friends.

If we begin to live in a reality of love shaped by a God who looks more like no-God than a traditional religious figure, maybe our expressions of faith can look more like no-faith than traditional religion.

Maybe faith is trusting that we are loved beyond all walls, beyond religion, and even beyond God.

Limitless

I've become pretty attached to calling myself a *runaway* as I've worked on this book. It's a concept I was proud of, one that had the power to explain so much, to reveal truths about faith, community, and the world we live in.

But as I wrestled with chapter after chapter, I began to have doubts that kept me up at night. By identifying as a runaway, was I avoiding a painful reality? Was I hiding from the truth instead of shining a light on it?

In a word, yes.

So here's the truth as I see it now. I hinted at it in part 4: The home I've always imagined returning to isn't there for me anymore. I'm no longer the boy who can run back from a cold, dark place to find the smell of warm bread and the sound of my father's harmonica welcoming me back.

I learned the shattering truth through my sessions with Alice and Solomon and even earlier, when I read Girard for the first time, but I wanted to forget it.

I didn't run away. I was kicked out.

When I visit my parents, I can now put a name to some of the grief and yearning I feel. And I know that becoming a runaway wasn't my choice.

I had no choice but to run when I found God outside the walls of my church home and turned around to discover I wasn't allowed to go back. I was only welcome if I continued to prop up the fortress walls that seemed to get higher and stronger every day to keep more people out.

From the outside, I no longer saw the walls as a source of safety, insulating me and my community from the harsh world outside. It now seemed that my family and community had drawn a perimeter around God's love, limiting it into a specific shape and form that I knew was a lie.

For those of you reading this because you see yourselves as runaways, here are three more truths:

God's love is limitless and unbounded.

If your family and community put limits and boundaries on their love, it's not love.

There is a world of love beyond the walls your family and friends keep shoring up with such determination, but you can step into that world only after facing and reckoning with the grief of losing those who taught you what love is.

Yes

Despite having written a whole book about it, I still don't have a lot of answers about what faith is, but I keep coming back to Jesus's metaphor of a seed. And I still like the idea of myself and all of us *being the seeds* because it requires us to look at the environment around us and ask hard questions.

"Is this an environment where this little seed can be nourished? Is this an environment where I can be nourished?"

Maybe another aspect of faith is believing that nourishing environments are out there, even if we've had only a small taste of nourishment up until this point.

Maybe faith is also recognizing we've been caught up in an environment of violence, an environment that pits us against each other so fiercely that we derive our sense of goodness and badness from these battles.

Maybe faith is letting go of the need to be "good" and voices that tell us we're "bad."

Maybe faith is knowing the only question that's important is the one Jesus points us to again and again: "Am I loved?"

Maybe faith is trusting that the answer is yes, even as we struggle to let go of the urge to *prove* our loveliness and worthiness.

Maybe faith is learning that the burden of love is light. We don't have to do anything to be loved, but in an environment of love, we can do everything.

Maybe faith is knowing there are no insiders or outsiders because there is no inside or outside.

Do you see the shift? It's about desire and identity.

It's a shift away from having to show evidence of our faith, striving, prostrating ourselves, and doing all the right things to receive our identities from someone else. It's a shift toward the God without vengeance, without rivalry, who simply shows us again and again and again that our identity is love.

I now believe that faith frees us up to be more human by confirming that nothing, *nothing*, can separate us from love.

I also believe that faith allows us to speak the truth about our own pain, freeing us from having to protect the goodness or badness of the people who hurt us. And it helps us find people who can hear our pain and attune to it, contain it, and hold us as we stitch up our wounds.

Faith is letting go of certainty, letting those concrete boxes crack wide open and crumble into gravel, then dust. Knowing that soon the dust will be swept up by a familiar warm breeze and scattered across a wide, green meadow where new things will grow.

Afterword

A few months ago, I got an email from a man named Edafe Okporo asking if I'd consider featuring him on my podcast. He had a new memoir coming out. I get these kinds of emails all the time, and it's rare that one jumps out and grabs me, but Mr. Okporo's did.

I googled his name and learned that his book, *Asylum: A Memoir & Manifesto*, was about growing up in Nigeria and eventually realizing he was gay. Edafe became a pastor to serve his community but had to flee to the United States when that community discovered he was gay, turned against him, and put him in danger. Edafe now works in New York City helping displaced people—particularly LGBTQ+ people. He is an educator and an advocate for immigration reform.

His moving, human story is about searching for a home and finding faith in new places.

As I read his manuscript, this story that is so very different from my own felt familiar on an elemental level. I read the final page again and again:

> *In the last few years, I have been asked, "Where are you from?"*
> *I answer, "Nigeria."*
> *And then people tell me I am far away from home.*

But my response is always the same: This is home for me now. Home is not just where you feel safe and welcome. It is also about how you can make it feel safe and welcoming for others.[1]

When I read Edafe's final lines, something hit me and helped me finish this book. His definition of home was what I'd been looking for.

I want to help create a place where *everyone* feels safe, welcome, and at peace—not in some cheery "everyone is welcome" kind of way—but in a way that's grounded in love and what love requires of us.

People often ask me if I still have faith. And for a long time, I wasn't sure.

Now I say *yes*.

Because faith is believing that getting to a place where we are all safe, welcome, and at peace is possible—despite the continued reality of oppression and injustice. And I'm a believer, even if it feels foolish many days.

But it's not only believing—it's also doing. Doing our part to create a home for ourselves and the people around us.

We have to recognize that when others are suffering, we are suffering. And instead of just singing, "It is well," as people of faith, we can shout, "It is not well," and we can then do something about it.

In taking action, we follow Jesus's example and truly become holy runaways.

I know now that I can tap into peace wherever I go, even as I, we, work to create a home where other runaways like me can come in from the cold and feel safe, welcome, and at peace.

A place where we can all sing together, "It is well. It is well with my soul."

Acknowledgments

So many people have contributed to a process that overwhelmingly consisted of me sitting on my floor, laptop propped on my coffee table, trying to write about God while muttering, "You really have gotten yourself into a mess this time, haven't you?"

To the laptop repair people who saved this book when I spilled coffee all over said laptop propped on my coffee table, thank you. You'll be thrilled to learn there are technically thousands of physical backups now.

Shelley Sperry, from the moment I called you with the idea for this book to the last round of edits, you've been an integral part of the creation of *Holy Runaways*. Your patient brilliance, endless responsiveness to phone calls and emails, and many hours you spent pouring over my words and ideas have crafted this into something far more beautiful than I'm capable of creating by myself. Thanks for tending well to this book alongside me over the nearly four years we've spent on it.

My agent, Rachelle Gardner. We've come a long way since twenty-four-year-old me emailed you an idea for a book called *Jesus Is My Boyfriend*, and you said, "Nope." Thank you for finally saying yes. I'm grateful for your wisdom and the ways you advocate on my behalf. I can't wait to do this again!

Lisa Kloskin, my editor, you're the reason I can even call myself an author. You are an example to me of what it means to live out my values through action instead of just saying them. Thank you for the ways you gently challenge me and for taking on another book from me. You open doors to so many people who don't often have opportunity in publishing, and I think that's neat.

To the team at Broadleaf Books, it's fun to be published by a press that I feel proud to associate with. Thank you for all the time and effort you have put into making this book a success.

Jen Hatmaker, I've felt you champion me ever since the first time you gave me a great big hug. Thank you for the foreword. Thank you for using your platform to uplift others. And thank you for modeling how to be a real person in the face of an industry where it's really easy to put on a mask.

Fr. James Alison, Abby Wong-Heffter, Dr. Angela Parker, Dr. O'Donnell Day, Rachael Clinton Chen, and Dr. Chelle Stearns, thank you not only for being such wise presences in my life but also for taking the time to read through draft sections of this manuscript to fact-check and help ensure I was on the right track. Your fingerprints are all over this book.

Roberto Ché Espinoza, Matthew Paul Turner, and Jonathan Merritt, your guidance was invaluable when I realized "I think I might need an agent!"

Jill Dyer and Paul Ritchie, there's something special about the tangible, physical support you both provided while I was writing. I've felt deeply cared for by you both. Thank you.

Riley Hall, Tamasin Thomas, Lizz Weaver, Kalee Vandegrift-Porter, Lora Kelley: you sipped wine while listening to me read early drafts of this book and said, "Sure!" every time I asked if you want to hear more. If you got bored, you didn't show it. (Well, Riley did once, but that section is fixed now.)

John Keatley, your photography is stunning.

There are so many more: Jeremiah and Jesse, Caleb, Riley, Pio, Joshua, Andrew, Abi, Kevin, Crystal, Cooper and Emily, Michael, Myles, Lauren, Tammy, Sergio, Kellye, Palmer, Jen and Kaz, Alejandra, Mari, Audrey, Torri and Alex, Scott, Kj, Kirk and Amy, Trapper. You've each contributed in different ways to keeping me balanced and (mostly) in reality while trying to write another book. In a pandemic. I'm grateful for the ways you bring your presence to my life, and I'm lucky to be surrounded by such incredible people I get to call my friends.

Anna, Jordan, Ella, Laurel, Mikayla, David, Mom, Dad. I love you.

Beatrice Rose, your huffs of disgust got me out of my chair and on much-needed walks. Yes, we can go to the park now.

Notes

Bigger

1 Matthew 17:20.

Exodus

1 Jeffrey M. Jones, "U.S. Church Membership Down Sharply in Past Two Decades," Gallup, April 18, 2019, https://news.gallup.com /poll/248837/church-membership-down-sharply-past-two-decades .aspx.

Faithless

1 Matthew 17:17.

Worthiness

1 Brené Brown, *The Gifts of Imperfection: Let Go of Who You Think You're Supposed to Be and Embrace Who You Are* (Center City, MN: Hazelden Publishing, 2010), 23.

Pressure

1 After reviewing recordings of the shootings and many in-depth interviews of witnesses, the FBI determined that the alleged exchange between Bernall and the shooter never actually happened. See

Alyssa Wilkinson, "After Columbine, Martyrdom Became a Powerful Fantasy for Christian Teenagers," *Vox*, April 17, 2019, https://www.vox.com/culture/2017/4/20/15369442/columbine-anniversary-cassie-bernall-rachel-scott-martyrdom.

Compression

1   "Seattle Super Bridge," *Impossible Engineering*, season 8, episode 2. First aired July 22, 2020.

Dangerous Virtues

1   Joe Rigney, "Do You Feel My Pain? Empathy, Sympathy, and Dangerous Virtues," *desiringGod*, May 2, 2020, https://www.desiringgod.org/articles/do-you-feel-my-pain.
2   Joe Rigney, "The Enticing Sin of Empathy," *desiringGod*, May 31, 2019, https://www.desiringgod.org/articles/the-enticing-sin-of-empathy.
3   Rigney, "Enticing Sin."
4   Rigney, "Enticing Sin."

Hot Coffee

1   See, for example, "The McDonald's Hot Coffee Case," Consumer Attorneys of California, https://www.caoc.org/?pg=facts.

Seeds

1   Charles Darwin, *The Origin of Species* (New York: Collier Press, 1909), 409.

Fertilizer

1   I pull a lot of this definition from Brené Brown's work. See Brené Brown, "Listening to Shame," filmed March 2012 in Long Beach, CA, TED video, 20:31, https://tinyurl.com/ngtbqqp.
2   Kristen Neff, *Self-Compassion: The Proven Power of Being Kind to Yourself* (New York: William Morrow, 2011), 160.
3   Neff, *Self-Compassion*, 162.

Windows

See R. M. Buijs, "The Autonomic Nervous System: A Balancing Act," *Handbook of Clinical Neurology* 117:1–11, https://doi.org/10.1016/B978-0-444-53491-0.00001-8.
2 Daniel J. Siegel, *The Developing Mind: How Relationships and the Brain Interact to Shape Who We Are*, 3rd ed. (New York: Guilford Press, 2020), 341–349.
3 Hillary L. McBride, *The Wisdom of Your Body: Finding Healing, Wholeness, and Connection through Embodied Living* (Grand Rapids, MI: Brazos, 2021), 67.
4 McBride, *The Wisdom of Your Body*, 67–68.
5 https://twitter.com/hillarylmcbride/status/1511146972341682176?s=20&t=eRljVNlbDhl_r598NiIlMQ.

Lizards

1 Resmaa Menakem, *My Grandmother's Hands: Racialized Trauma and the Pathway to Mending Our Hearts and Bodies* (Las Vegas, NV: Central Recovery Press, 2017), 6.
2 Menakem, *My Grandmother's Hands*, 6.

Desire

1 Chelle Stearns, Lecture in Faith, Hope, and Love, The Seattle School of Theology and Psychology, September 15, 2014.
2 Sarah Coakley, *God, Sexuality, and the Self: An Essay "On the Trinity"* (New York: Cambridge University Press, 2013), 10.
3 Coakley, *God, Sexuality*, 10.

Stepping Stones

1 "Nadia Bolz-Weber Is Trying Compassion," Queerology, episode 97, May 5, 2020.
2 "Nadia Bolz-Weber Is Trying Compassion."

I See It, I Want It

1 René Girard, *Deceit, Desire, and the Novel* (Baltimore: Johns Hopkins Press, 1965), 2.

Neurons

1 Vittorio Gallese, Luciano Fadiga, Leonardo Fogassi, and Giacomo Rizzolatti, "Action Recognition in the Premotor Cortex," *Brain* 119 (1996): 593–609.
2 Siegel, *The Developing Mind*, 251–252.

Mind

1 Siegel, *The Developing Mind*, 5.
2 Menakem, *My Grandmother's Hands*, 152.

Boots

1 Angela N. Parker, *If God Still Breathes, Why Can't I?: Black Lives Matter and Biblical Authority* (Grand Rapids, MI: Wm. B. Eerdmans Publishing, 2021), 33.
2 Parker, *If God Still Breathes*, 34.

Scapegoats

1 For one description and interpretation of this, see Rabbi Jonathan Sacks, "The Scapegoat: Atonement and Purification," Chabad-Lubavitch Media Center, chabad.org, https://www.chabad.org/parshah/article_cdo/aid/1846869/jewish/The-Scapegoat-Atonement-and-Purification.htm.
2 See Ronald Takai, *A Different Mirror: A History of Multicultural America*, rev. ed. (New York: Back Bay Books, 2008), 23–48; David Silverman, *This Land Is Their Land: The Wampanoag Indians, Plymouth Colony, and the Troubled History of Thanksgiving* (New York: Bloomsbury, 2019).

Myths

1 https://www.cnn.com/2001/US/09/14/Falwell.apology/.
2 https://www.cnn.com/2001/US/09/14/Falwell.apology/.
3 Michael Kirwan, *Discovering Girard* (Lanham, MD: Cowley Publications, 2005), 54.